WHO PAYS FOR CAR ACCID

The Fault versus No-Fault Insuranc

Controversies in Public Policy
edited by Rita J. Simon

Previous titles in this series

The Privatization of Policing: Two Views
Brian Forst and Peter K. Manning

Does Family Preservation Serve a Child's Best Interests?
Howard Altstein and Ruth G. McRoy

Women in Combat: Civic Duty or Military Liability?
Lorry M. Fenner and Marie E. deYoung

WHO PAYS FOR CAR ACCIDENTS?

The Fault versus No-Fault Insurance Debate

Jerry J. Phillips
Stephen Chippendale

Georgetown University Press/Washington, D.C.

Georgetown University Press, Washington, D.C. 20007
© 2002 by Georgetown University Press. All rights reserved.
Printed in the United States of America
10 9 8 7 6 5 4 3 2 1   2002
This volume is printed on acid-free offset book paper.

Library of Congress Cataloging-in-Publication Data

Phillips, Jerry J., 1935–
    Who pays for car accidents? : the fault versus no-fault insurance debate /
Jerry Phillips and Stephen Chippendale.
        p. cm. — (Controversies in public policy)
    Includes bibliographical references (p.) and index.
    ISBN 0-87840-887-8 (pbk. : alk. paper)
    1. Insurance, No-fault automobile—United States. 2. Traffic accidents.
I. Chippendale, Stephen. II. Title. III. Series.

HG9970.3 .P49 2002
368.5'728—dc21   2001040802

Contents

List of Tables

About the Authors

Stephen Chippendale, a University of Minnesota law graduate, currently practices law at Cadwalader, Wickersham, and Taft in Washington, D.C.

Jerry J. Phillips is a professor at the University of Tennessee law school.

Preface

Two lawyers, one a professor, the other a practicing attorney, debate fault versus no-fault auto insurance in the fourth volume of our Controversies in Public Policy series.

Practicing attorney Steve Chippendale argues in favor of no-fault reform primarily for the following reasons: The fault system is costly, inefficient, and time consuming. Under the fault system, the lawyers involved are the primary beneficiaries. The plaintiffs' lawyers, who usually work on a contingency-fee basis, take one-third of their party's recovery, and the defense attorneys are paid on an hourly basis. Payments for pain and suffering under the fault system drive up insurance costs. Excessive litigation leads to higher premiums even though safer cars are being produced and fewer accidents are occurring on the roads. Chippendale also supports a variation of no fault authored by Jeffrey O'Connell and Michael Horowitz, which he describes as "auto choice." Auto choice gives motorists a choice between being eligible for damages resulting from pain and suffering or forgoing such claims.

University of Tennessee law professor Jerry Phillips argues in favor of the fault system currently in use in thirty-seven states, stating that the dual goals of automobile tort law are to compensate the injured and to deter drivers who are at fault. Phillips believes that it contains all the advantages and is clearly preferable to any no-fault system. The debate between fault and no fault, Phillips states, hinges basically on a determination of five policy issues: cost, expedition, fault determination, deterrence, and compensation. In his essay, Phillips considers all of these issues and comes out in favor of the tort system and fault liability.

More so than in several of the earlier pro and con volumes, the authors of this one grant a good deal of respect for the other's position and recommend acceptance of some of the ingredients of the other's case. Phillips recommends some compromise on the traditional tort system, and Chippendale believes adoption of auto choice gives plaintiffs an opportunity to recover losses as a result of "pain and suffering." Readers will be exposed to thorough, incisive arguments for and against tort liability that are made by the legal scholars in this volume.

Rita J. Simon
Series Editor

PART ONE

Jerry J. Phillips
The Case for Automobile Tort Liability

☐ 1. NO FAULT OR TORT?

As with almost all issues, resolution of the issue of whether to have no fault or tort coverage for automobile accidents depends on how the question is asked. One way to phrase the question is, do we want no-fault compensation for injuries resulting from automobile accidents? Another is, do we want to have tort liability for accidents caused by the fault of another?

The two questions do not entail mutually exclusive answers. That is to say, a jurisdiction can have both no-fault compensation and tort liability. Indeed, eight American states have just such a system of mandatory add-on, no-fault auto liability (Dewees, Duff, and Trebilcock 1996, 22). Moreover, auto-liability insurance policies typically provide for no-fault, first-party medical insurance, although the amount of such coverage is usually small. In addition, many persons have collateral public or private insurance coverage for medical expenses and lost wages caused by illness or accidents, including automobile accidents.

The answers to the questions may, however, be mutually exclusive, either in whole or in part. Quebec has pure no-fault auto insurance, to the virtual exclusion of auto-tort liability (Joost 1999, § 7.5), and New Zealand has a general system of government-sponsored accident compensation to the virtual exclusion of tort liability (Mahoney 1992, 159).

Twelve U.S. states, on the other hand, have a mandatory partial, exclusive no-fault system up to a certain level, or threshold—usually defined in terms of medical expenses incurred, or in terms of seriousness of the injury—and beyond that threshold, the accident victim must sue in tort (Dewees, Duff, and Trebilcock 1996, 22). This threshold system was proposed by Robert Keeton and Jeffrey O'Connell in their 1965 book, *Basic Protection for the Traffic Victim*. This system can be justified on the grounds of taking relatively small claims, that tend to clog the courts, out of the judicial system (since no fault should normally be handled administratively, without the necessity of a lawsuit); assuring some compensation in all cases (assuming no fault is paid up to the threshold even when a serious injury occurs); and providing a compromise, for those who insist that tort law should be retained at least for the serious injuries. The threshold plans exclude only personal injuries, and not property-damage claims, on the assumption that property claims usually get disposed of expeditiously under the tort system.

A final form of no-fault insurance is elective, or optional, no fault. Three American states have optional, threshold no fault (Dewees, Duff, and Trebilcock 1996, 22). Proposals by Jeffrey O'Connell (1990, 947) and in

Congress would permit broader no-fault election by individual choice. One who elects no fault normally could not sue or be sued in tort, and one who elects tort normally could only sue or be sued in tort by another tort elector in the applicable jurisdiction. The elective no-fault proposal raises questions about the type of drivers who would elect no fault, and about the effect of no-fault elections on those who elect tort.

The rule in effect in the majority of U.S. jurisdictions is that of tort liability for automobile injuries (Joost 1992, § 7.5). An accident victim generally cannot recover against another unless the other is at fault in causing the accident. In some instances the car manufacturer may be responsible for the accident and can be sued in strict tort (Phillips 1998). In most U.S. jurisdictions the victim's fault will reduce rather than bar her recovery (Phillips, Terry, Maraist, and McClellan 1997, 639). As noted above, in a tort jurisdiction there may also be no-fault sources of recovery available to the accident victim either through public or private insurance.

In making a choice between fault and no fault, basically five policy issues are at stake: (1) cost; (2) expedition; (3) fault determination; (4) deterrence; and (5) compensation. The no-fault proponents assert that no-fault auto accident coverage is less expensive than tort, in terms of insurance costs, and that it is more expeditious in that claims get paid more quickly. They claim that tort law is ineffective because it rests on proof of fault, which is problematical in many if not most cases. They claim that it is very doubtful whether tort liability for auto accidents effectively achieves one of its primary goals of tort deterrence, and they claim that no fault much more effectively achieves the other primary tort goal of compensation. The debate on the choice between auto no fault and tort liability basically hinges on a determination of these five issues.

Once again, however, everything depends on how you pose the issue, or frame the question. How costly a no-fault plan will be depends on the size of deductibles and benefits received, as well as on the effectiveness with which the insurance industry is regulated. Expeditiousness may not be a desideratum, if a claimant has adequate financial resources so as to be able to weather a tort determination. There is considerable dispute over whether tort law adequately determines fault and adequately deters. Finally, tort liability may not exist primarily to compensate, especially where alternative modes of private or public compensation are or should be in place.

There is yet another underpinning of tort liability. It has been persuasively contended that the tort remedy provides one with a feeling of vindication, and with the right to be heard, which are very valuable attributes whether one wins or loses (Phillips 1985). Over against this contention is the assertion that many people are dissatisfied with the judicial system, particularly with tort litigation (Bell and O'Connell 1997; Harper, James, and Gray 1986, § 13.8), and the admonition of Judge Learned Hand (1926, 105) that most people fear litigation like the plague.

A major component in the tort–no fault debate is the appropriate rules of damages. No fault usually does not fully compensate, providing only partial wage and medical recovery and caps on the total amount of recovery (Joost 1999, chapter 6). There are also legislative tort caps in some states, but a number of these caps have been struck down as unconstitutional (*Best v. Taylor Machine Works*, 179 Ill. 2d 367, 689 N. E. 2d 1057 (1997); Schwartz 1997). No fault does not provide for punitive damages, although egregious conduct such as wantonness and drunken driving may be sufficient to remove no-fault coverage and allow for tort liability including punitive damages (*Pinnick v. Cleary*, 360 Mass. 1, 271 N. E. 2d 592, n. 13 (1971); Schermer 1995, § 8.01).

No-fault coverage typically does not allow recovery for so-called nonpecuniary damages, such as pain and suffering and mental distress. The reason for this exclusion is apparently because such damages are not readily calculable, and would complicate the administrative process. There is probably also a belief that nonpecuniary damages are not real damages—although the trend of modern tort law is toward the greater recognition of such damages as a legitimate basis of recovery (Phillips, Terry, Maraist, and McClellan 1997, chapter 21).

No-fault plans also generally reject the collateral source rule.[1] That is, if an injured party is covered by public or private insurance, payments under such insurance for medical expenses and lost wages should be credited against the no-fault coverage—rather than treated as additional payments, as the collateral source rule does. No-fault proponents contend that the collateral source rule permits double recovery, and is economically inefficient. Tort proponents contend that the rule supports full recovery, individual thrift, and internalization of accident costs.

All these issues are considered in more depth below.

In the best of all worlds, probably an add-on system would be preferable. Under this system, the auto accident victim could be assured of some reasonable compensation, while the goals of the tort system could also be vindicated. Some believe such a dual system would be too expensive, especially if the no-fault coverage were generous and if both no-fault and tort-liability coverage were made compulsory as a condition to owning an automobile. The cost argument is met with the counterargument that automobile operation should be made to pay its own way, and that automobiles should not be operated by financially irresponsible drivers.

In the event that, for whatever reason, a choice must be made between no-fault and tort liability for automobile accidents, the balance of policy considerations appears to weigh in favor of tort liability. Tort law is based on individual responsibility. It provides fuller coverage, where liability is warranted. No fault points toward a system of assured compensation, which is a suitable, public policy government initiative and which is in no way restricted in its policy implications to automobile accidents (Blum and Kalven 1965, 83). Apart from auto accidents, governmentally provided health insurance for everyone is long overdue in this country. Those who are employed should be provided reasonable unemployment compensation by their employers for sickness or injury.

☐ 2. THE DETERMINATION OF FAULT

Jeffrey O'Connell (1975) has been a foremost proponent of the idea that a determination of fault in the automobile accident context is largely a matter of guesswork. Terence Ison (1967) refers to the fault determination as a lottery—a game of chance. Obviously, if this criticism is valid, there is little justification for retaining the tort system as the basis of recovery for automobile accidents, because tort liability depends on proof of fault.

Empirical studies indicate, however, that fault can be reasonably allocated in a much higher number of auto accident cases than critics suggest. In a study of 352 insurance claims in 1968, Franklin J. Marryott "found that there was some question concerning fault in only 7.4 percent of cases. He also found that there was clear evidence of fault in 90.6 percent of the 106 bodily injury cases" (in Bruce 1984, 69). He reported that six experienced claims adjusters estimated that 75 percent of cases "were susceptible of clear determinations on the original reports and about 90 percent upon the completion of the initial investigation" (Bruce 1984, 69).

There are several recurring fault indicators associated with automobile accidents. One such indicator is speeding. "Repeated experiments have shown the increases in the speed at which automobiles are driven will be associated with higher incidences of accidents" (Bruce 1984, 70).

"Even more impressive is the evidence that driving while intoxicated is a cause of accidents." One study showed "that 44.3 percent of 7,292 fatally injured drivers in the United States had blood alcohol concentrations . . . in excess of 0.10 percent" (Bruce 1984, 70). Another study showed "that 77 percent of 208 drivers killed in single vehicle accidents in New York had been drinking" (Bruce 1984, 70). In an often-quoted study cited by Bruce (p. 70), Borkenstein et al. found that the probability of causing a collision when driving with a blood alcohol content of 0.10 percent "was 6 or 7 times greater than if the driver had not been drinking and at 0.15 or over the probability was 24 times as great."

Failure to wear seat belts has been "conclusive[ly]" shown to produce a dramatic increase in injuries and deaths. "For example, in a study of 28,780 accidents involving Volvo drivers it was found that the injury rate among front seat occupants fell from 1,514 per 10,000 accidents to 725 if seat belts were worn, and that the fatality rate fell from 41 per 10,000 to 4" (Bruce 1984, 70). The law in the United States varies widely, however, as to whether failure to wear an available seat belt constitutes legal fault (Dobbs 2000, § 205), and any determination of fault in this regard is further complicated by the required presence of air bags at both the driver's and the front seat passenger's seating positions for cars manufactured after 1 September 1997 (U.S. Department of Transportation 1993, 46,551).[2]

There is evidence that the commission of traffic offenses is related to the incidence of automobile accidents. Ignoring stop signs, failing to yield the right-of-way, and tailgating are common among such offenses (Bruce 1984, 72).

Finally, the very high rate of settlement of automobile accident cases indicates that fault is not difficult to determine, since presumably most of the cases would not settle unless the presence or absence of fault could be determined. As Bruce noted:

> Further evidence of the relative non-controversiality of fault determination comes from the very high percentage of automobile accident cases which are settled out of court. In a study of 86,100 personal injuries, for example, Conard et al. found that only 14 percent of those involved considered there to be sufficient dispute over any issue to hire a lawyer; that less than 0.6 percent of all cases were sufficiently complex that they had to be settled by the courts; and that only 5 percent of the serious injury cases had to be settled in court. Similarly, in a study of more than 300 automobile accident cases reported to British solicitors, Ison (1967: 153) found that only 5 percent went to trial. And Zeisel et al. (1959) concluded that in the United States only 2 or 3 percent of all personal injury claims ever reached the stage where they were decided by the judgement of a jury or a court (Bruce 1984, 72).[3]

The critics of the auto system of fault liability contend that driving is too complex for fault to be determined with any certainty in the average case. For example, in an often-cited quote, Leon Green (1958, 66–68) said the driver

. . . must observe the operation of other vehicles, front and rear and to the sides—those he is meeting, those that pass, and those that may cross his path. He must observe road signs, stop signs, cautions, traffic lines, light signals and watch for signals of other motorists and give proper signals himself. He must know the operating mechanisms of his machine, check their operations as he travels, and maintain his rapidly moving and complex machine under control at all times. . . . Multiply the same duties and hazards by any number of other operators in the immediate vicinity; add the duties and hazards of highway maintenance, passengers, pedestrians, and adjacent landowners, the conduct of any one or more of whom may impose upon all operators in close proximity duties and hazards requiring instant and perhaps unerring judgment and action. Add further the hazards of climatic condition; the imperfections of the human being in sight, judgment, muscular reaction, health, strength, and experience. Bring any combination of these duties and hazards into focus on a collision at high speed at a particular point of time and place. Who can name all the factors involved in causing the collision?

To the difficulty of fault determination, Green (1958, 66–68) adds the difficulty of fact determination:

. . . Who in retrospect from the tangled fragments of evidence given by the participants or by-standers and those who arrived on the scene at a later time; from marks and measurements, calculations of time and speed, is expert enough to reconstruct the fleeting scene with any assurance of its accuracy?

B. Dunlop and William Prosser reflect this view of the difficulty of fact determination. Dunlop (1975, 447) says:

Motor vehicle accidents are events which occur suddenly, taking the witnesses, including the participants, by surprise and resulting in imperfect perception. Months, even years, after the event, they are called upon to assess distances, relative speeds, time elapsed: all matters as to which they have little or no experience.

Prosser echoes this view:

. . . [E]vidence given in personal injury cases usually consists of highly contradictory statements from the two sides, estimating such factors as time, speed, distance and visibility, offered months after the event by witnesses who were never very sure just what happened when they saw it, and whose faulty memories are undermined by lapse of time, by bias, by conversations with others, and by the subtle influence of counsel (in Rokes 1971, 138).

Insofar as observation, memory, and bias affect the reliability of eyewitness testimony, auto-tort litigation reflects problems that are typical of trial litigation. The other charge—that driving is too complex a task to be performed safely—is belied by the fact that tens of millions of people perform the task safely every day. The implied argument that inadvertence or inattention does not constitute fault, cuts much too far. Negligence consists of inadvertence or inattention.

There is a trend in the products liability field to say that mere inadvertence or inattention does not constitute contributory fault, especially in the context of workplace injuries (Phillips 1998, 276–77). This doctrine has not typically been extended beyond the products area. It is applied in the products liability context as a matter of policy, on the rationale that the product supplier is in a better position to prevent the injury, and that from a human factors perspective such inadvertence and inattention are readily foreseeable and largely unpreventable by the consumer. This rationale does not apply between two drivers, or between a driver and pedestrian. If, however, a jury believes that a person's inadvertence or inattention does not constitute legal fault on the facts of a given case, then they are at liberty to find that person free of fault.

❑ 3. TORT DETERRENCE AND RELATED GOALS

There are three major arguments directed against tort liability as an effective deterrent of auto injuries and deaths: (1) The fear for one's own safety is a sufficient deterrent to careless driving, so that the additional threat of tort liability will have little if any increased deterrent effect on the driver; (2) Many, if not most, auto accidents are caused by inadvertence and inattention, which are not effectively susceptible to deterrence through the threat of tort liability; and (3) The availability of liability insurance essentially blunts any concern for personal responsibility which might give rise to deterrence.

Each of these arguments will be addressed in turn. In connection with the third argument, there is a related concern of whether tort liability with insurance is any greater a deterrent than no-fault liability with insurance. In other words, does the ready availability of insurance in both tort and no-fault liability neutralize any difference between the two systems of liability, insofar as deterrence is concerned?

Finally, one must ask whether auto-tort liability serves societal goals not served by no fault.

Fear for One's Own Safety

Christopher J. Bruce makes the economic argument that the threat of tort liability may increase driver caution, over and above the degree of caution already provided by the fear of self-injury to the driver as a result of careless driving. He first notes the arguments against increased caution through threat of tort liability, as expressed by S. L. Kimball, P. S. Atiyah, and W. J. Blum and H. Kalven. Kimball says:

> Fear of injury to oneself, habits of caution, concern for the trouble one might have if involved in an accident, even innocently, simple human decency are all deterrents far more potent than potential liability for fault (in Bruce 1984, 78).

Atiyah states the argument in the context of contributory negligence as a bar:

> The instinct for self-preservation is plainly so powerful in all ordinary people that if it fails to deter a person from doing something which may cause him injury, it is barely conceivable that he could be deterred by threatening to deprive him of compensation (in Bruce 1984, 78).

As Blum and Kalven (1967, 254) put the matter:

> It is surely commonplace knowledge that any driver is always risking not simply the safety of others, but equally his own personal safety. Inasmuch as the situation thus already seems to present a very high inducement to safety, it is hard to see what additional incentive to super-care will be added by economic pressure.

Bruce (1984, 79) responds:

> Thus, they are led to hypothesise, in effect, that an increase in the price of accident-causing behavior can have no effect on that behavior. Yet one of the most soundly-based hypotheses in economic theory is that an increase in the price of an activity will lead, ceteris paribus, to a reduction in the demand for that activity.

It might be argued, Bruce continues, that since the risk of accident-causing behavior may be death, "any *incremental* penalty would be, relatively, small" (emphasis added). However, he says, this argument "fails to recognize that the expected cost of any individual unsafe act is not the value associated with the life that might be lost, but that value multiplied by the probability that a fatal accident would occur." Since the risk of a fatal accident is small, and perceived as such, therefore that risk may not have much deterrent effect on careless driving. Bruce concludes by noting that the scientific evidence indicates "drivers *will* respond to the threat of financial penalties by altering certain types of behavior" (Bruce 1984, 84; emphasis added).

Gary Schwartz (1994, 383) acerbically addresses the question of whether one's moral concern for the safety of others is a sufficient deterrent to prevent accidents. "Many of the motorists one encounters on the highway," he says, "do not seem greatly concerned about the welfare of others."

Inadvertence and Inattention

It has been argued that accidents frequently result from "momentary inadvertence, forgetfulness, or lack or foresight that is part of the normal routine of everyday life" (Ison 1967, 8), and that such accidents cannot realistically be avoided. In other words, inadvertence is an inherent human response that cannot be deterred. As a corollary, some argue that driving is such a difficult task that it will not be possible for drivers to avoid causing accidents (Platt 1962).

Bruce concludes, based on "the available scientific evidence," that the "driving task is sufficiently straight-forward [so] that it can be mastered without difficulty by the vast majority of individuals" (Bruce 1984, 76). In his view, individuals who "cause accidents because they were inattentive, made miscalculations, allowed their minds to wander, or tried a maneuver which was beyond their level of competency can be induced to alter their behavior if they are made aware of the consequences of their actions" (Bruce 1984, 77–78). Even though there may be "some types of accidents which, reasonably, may be said to be 'unavoidable,'" he says, the number of accidents that result from "conscious decisions to behave in an unsafe manner is sufficient that significant potential for the operation of the deterrent effect remains" (Bruce 1984, 78).

Schwartz echoes Bruce's conclusions. He believes that inadvertent negligence is "imperfectly deterrable." But it "does not follow," he says, "that this category of negligence is not deterrable at all." After all, most of us, appreciating that inadvertence can be disadvantageous, "adopt habits or 'scripts' that enable us to avoid inadvertence most of the time" (Schwartz 1994, 385–86). Moreover, he notes, speeding and drunk driving, which are often the cause of accidents, are frequently the result of conscious decisions that are within the driver's control (p. 386).

F. A. Sloan, B. A. Reilley, and C. M. Schenzler (1994, 68) concluded from reviewing the empirical studies that, overall, it appears that tort liability has a deterrent effect on careless driving. Their studies also led them to conclude that "tort liability rules . . . are more effective in reducing binge drinking [and driving] than are criminal sanctions" (Sloan, Reilley, and Schenzler 1995, 73).

Common sense as well as empirical studies support the conclusion that, while perhaps inadvertence itself cannot be deterred, the situations that lead to inadvertence can be. One can be deterred from driving while sleepy, from using a cellular telephone while driving,[4] and from becoming involved in many other distracting activities while driving. People are responsive to economic penalties, and tort law provides such an economic deterrence.

The Effect of Insurance

It has been contended that the deterrent effect of tort law is largely blunted by the widespread availability of automobile liability insurance. If the insurer, rather than the insured, pays for tortious injuries, the insured has no significant financial incentive to avoid liability. The cost of accidents is spread among all insureds, as a function of the insurance mechanism.

Relying on research conducted by Richard W. Grayston, Gary Schwartz concludes that tort liability does have a significant deterrent effect on the occurrence of auto accidents, even with the presence of liability insurance:

> Despite, then, an ample tort system, there is a very high volume of motorist negligence. It by no means follows, however, that the level of negligence would be no higher in the absence of tort liability. A 1972 study by Grayston reached two empirical findings. First, higher premiums for auto liability insurance decrease the number of drivers, and hence the number of highway injuries and fatalities, most of which are of course due to motorist negligence. This finding suggests how a negligence liability rule interacts with liability insurance to produce a strict-liability-like effect that regulates the decisions of actors to engage in dangerous activities. Grayston's second finding is that the more state regulators permit practices such as class rating and merit rating, the lower the number of accidents and injuries (Schwartz 1994, 393–94).

While the insured does not feel the direct or immediate financial impact of tort liability if she is insured, that impact will take effect when insurance premiums are adjusted to reflect the effect of tort liability.

What, then, is the effect of the adoption of no fault? Specifically, does it decrease the deterrent effect of insurance?

A number of studies indicate that the change from tort to no fault does decrease the insurance deterrent effect. Elizabeth Landes estimates that "states which place relatively moderate restrictions on tort suits have had between 2 and 5 percent more fatal accidents as a result of adopting no-fault, while states with more restrictive laws have had as many as 10–15 percent more fatal accidents" (Landes 1982, 50). D. Dewees, D. Duff, and M. Trebilcock (1996, 22–25) review the various studies that compare no fault with tort and that conclude no fault decreases the deterrent effect as compared to tort. They note that these studies have been criticized on methodological grounds. Schwartz (1994, 394–96) also reviews these studies and the various criticisms that have been made.

Bruce (1984, 87), reviewing the statistical work of Richard Grayston, notes the latter's conclusion "that when 21 American states introduced 'merit rating' schemes in the early 1960s, they obtained significant reductions in both the number of accidents and the number of injuries per [car] registration."

Merit rating is a method by which a driver's at-fault accident record is reflected in the insurance premiums she must pay. A safe record entails low premiums, with concomitant higher premiums as the number of at-fault accidents increases. A carefully regulated merit-rating system should bring the deterrent effect of tort insurance fairly closely in line with the deterrent effect of tort liability.

Typically no-fault auto insurance is not merit rated.[5] If it were merit rated, no-fault insurance would essentially resemble tort liability insurance in its deterrent effect. The fault principle of tort liability, however, provides a stigma that is not attached to no fault and that may well deter without regard to the availability of insurance.

Related Goals

Even assuming auto-tort liability has no significant deterrent effect on some types of wrongful driver misconduct, it would still serve the substantial purpose of allocating liability to the wrongdoer. As noted above, the overwhelming majority of auto accidents can be reasonably determined on the basis of fault.

Tort law serves other valuable functions as well. "Lay juries," as Joseph Little (1989, 35, 38, 39) observes, act as "surrogates of the public conscience." Loss fixing "is done under the basic personal accountability and blameworthiness premises of tort law." Tort law is always in a process of evolution, and "true reform of tort law necessarily implies enhancing the goals of personal accountability and of self-governance."

Tort law, Marshall Shapo (1999, 1045) says, serves "as a social symbol, a cultural mirror that reflects the moral views of society." No fault, on the other hand, is an administrative remedy that is largely devoid of moral content. No fault may provide efficient minimum compensation, but it should not be allowed to do so at the cost of the public conscience that is represented by tort law.

The common-law tort system "represents an ideal scheme to protect the rights and interests of the common person." This ideal is often "flawed in practice, but nevertheless is cherished in our society." The system should not be dispensed with "except on clear and convincing proof of its inadequacy," and thus far that proof has not been presented (Phillips 1985, 615–16). Specifically, on balance auto-tort law appears to more closely reflect societal values than does no fault.

4. COMPENSATION

In General

Philosophically and practically the principal difference between no fault and tort auto liability is that no fault attempts to compensate a greater number of individuals, based on the occurrence of injury rather than on fault, while tort will likely compensate a smaller number of individuals since not all persons' accidents are caused by the fault of another. Conversely, payout under no fault is typically restricted, while tort liability is more generous and typically unlimited in amount (subject to the availability of assets and the reasonableness of the amount of damages).

In fact, the extent to which auto accident tort victims are left entirely uncompensated from any source is unclear. Early research by Conard et al. (cited in Keeton and O'Connell 1965, 48, 237) indicated that the immediate medical needs of auto accident victims "were almost always well met from one source or another," while long-range medical needs "were not provided for quite as well." These researchers also concluded that legal liability systems (including tort and workers' compensation), "despite all the controversy they engender, provide less than one-fourth of the sums provided by loss-insurance-type systems." Thus, private insurance, including unemployment insurance, may be providing a significant amount of cover for out-of-pocket losses without regard to auto-fault or no-fault liability.

The number of recoveries in tort varies dramatically depending on whether or not the auto tortfeasor has liability insurance. A Michigan study indicated that only 37 percent of auto accident victims received anything in tort, with 55 percent recovering in the event of death or serious injury (Keeton and O'Connell 1965, 49). A study by Clarence Morris and James Paul (cited by Keeton and O'Connell 1965, 50) similarly showed "that 54.6 percent of those in serious accident cases suffering personal injury or death received something in tort." On the other hand, the Columbia Report showed 87 percent of claimants recovering something in tort, and the Fleming James and Stewart Law Report showed a figure of 95-percent recovery, but these were "only for claims against *insured* defendants" (Keeton and O'Connell 1965, 51–52; emphasis in original).

Studies by the U.S. Bureau of Justice Statistics showed that plaintiffs were successful in 57.5 percent of the auto cases tried in state courts in 1996 (DeFrances and Litras 1999, 6), and in 58.8 percent of such cases tried in 1996 in federal court (Litras and DeFrances 1999, 5). State courts dispose of about seven times more civil cases than federal district courts (DeFrances and Litras 1999, 12).

This percentage of recovery in litigation does not indicate the true percentage of recovery, however. Walter J. Blum and Harry Kalven, Jr., in *Public Law Perspectives on a Private Law Problem: Auto Compensation Plans* (1965), noted that the new Columbia study showed that "less than 2%" of personal injury claims were "disposed of by trial" while "more than 98%" were "disposed of by settlement." These statistics are generally conceded to be fairly accurate. Moreover, apparently the overwhelming bulk of auto injuries result in claims. Relying on a study by Roger B. Hunting and Gloria S. Neuwirth, Blum and Kalven concluded that only about 13 percent of auto accident victims do not file a claim (p. 19).

Settlements will generally be for less than the amount of injuries claimed, since the nature of the settlement process is one of compromise. Settlements should not be decried for this reason, however, as long as they are arrived at by mutual consent after fair disclosure.

As is apparent from the above, the likelihood of auto-tort recovery is heavily dependent on the tortfeasor having liability insurance. Robert Joost (1999, § 1.8) states that as of 1999, "[f]orty of the 51 jurisdictions in the United States . . . require motorists to maintain [bodily injury] auto insurance." He concludes that it "has been difficult, if not impossible, to enforce this type of law," especially when drivers "have no licenses or registrations," are newly arrived or out-of-state residents, or "have allowed their insurance to lapse" (Joost 1992, § 1.8). This conclusion is not foregone, however. For example, in 1996 the State of California passed legislation requiring police, when stopping motorists, to ask for proof of insurance. If the motorist cannot comply, a heavy fine and license suspension can be imposed. If such a motorist is involved in an accident, he will be barred from recovering noneconomic losses in tort (Joost 1999, § 1.8). Financial responsibility laws may be difficult to enforce, but the result of the effort to enforce them would be well worth it.

Financial-responsibility or compulsory-liability-insurance laws quite generally have low required limits of coverage—$20,000 per individual, and $40,000 per accident are probably typical limits. Such limits are ridiculously low. Limits of $100,000 to $500,000 are more reasonable. Such limits would obviously make driving more expensive, but auto traffic is a social ill in many respects and should be discouraged in favor of alternative means of transportation. Moreover, there is indication of a significant correlation between uninsured drivers and careless drivers (Keeton and O'Connell 1965, 91). The more financially responsible drivers therefore are likely to be the safer drivers.

Insurance companies generally resist the adoption of compulsory-liability insurance laws. They offer a variety of reasons, but probably the central concern is that "turning insurance into a 'tax' on driving invites state intervention in—or indeed ownership of—the insurance business" (Keeton and O'Connell 1965, 92). This concern is contrary to the general inclination toward private insurance in this country. Interestingly, the insurance industry has shown no opposition to no fault—probably because no fault looks like a profitable venture to insurers. Keeton and O'Connell (1965, 91), however, argue that it is "unconscionable" for a driver to go uninsured, thereby forcing "others to depend on him to avoid accidents." The indefensibility of this position is especially acute, they say, since the uninsured is most likely to be the "financially irresponsible" and "the young," who "as a group not only have incomparably the worst driving habits but often drive the most dangerous cars" (see also *Tennessee Attorneys Memo* 2000, 1).

It is widely contended that smaller tort claims—however defined—are overcompensated, while serious and especially catastrophic injuries are undercompensated (Keeton and O'Connell 1965, 2). It is difficult to understand what is meant by overcompensation in this context. Probably some commentators refer to the recovery for pain and suffering and emotional distress, which is usually three or four times the amount of the out-of-pocket loss. Treating recovery for pain and suffering as overcompensation shows a bias against such damages. The catastrophically injured person frequently does not recover even out-of-pocket losses (Phillips, Terry, Maraist, and

McClellan 1997, 1407). But no fault does not remedy this situation, because of the limits in payment and coverage set by American no-fault plans (Schermer 1995, chapters 14, 63).

Pain and Suffering Damages

A favorite scapegoat for tort opponents is the item of recovery for pain and suffering damages and damages for mental distress. Many tort retrenchment statutes attempt to limit or exclude recovery for such damages (American Law Institute 1991, 203). Proponents of "tort reform" propose limiting or excluding such damages. No-fault auto plans almost universally deny recovery for such damages. Congress amended the Internal Revenue Code in 1996 to provide that tort recovery for emotional distress is taxable as income (U.S. Code 1996, 26, § 104(a)). This amendment may be unconstitutional as a direct tax on an item that is not income, but loss replacement (Hubbard 1998, 50).

This aversion to recovery for pain and suffering and mental distress—what can be described as dignitary injuries—is contrary to the trend in developing modern tort law (Shapo 1999). Dignitary injuries are becoming increasingly recognized as central items of damage—in civil rights claims, tortious invasions of the personality, toxic torts, and other vanguard areas of tort law development.

What are the objections to recovery for dignitary losses? One economic approach has been to argue that recovery for such damages should be disallowed because the average person, if given the choice, would not purchase pain and suffering insurance coverage for herself, apparently because that person would not consider such cover to be worth the price (Bell and O'Connell 1997, 223). This economic argument is dubious at best, since insurance companies do not offer such first-party coverage in the first place. In the one area where the motorist can purchase pain and suffering insurance coverage—in the form of uninsured and underinsured motorist coverage—the purchase of such insurance is widespread.

Another objection to recovery for pain and mental anguish is that such damages are too difficult to calculate—they are uncertain, subject to wide differences of calculation, and are likely to delay the settlement process. This objection seems unfounded, because something on the order of 98 percent of tort claims settle. An accomplished trial attorney can estimate fairly accurately the high and low values of an auto accident claim. The rule of thumb of three to four times out-of-pocket damages seems to work pretty well in the majority of cases as a rough way of calculating noneconomic loss. For those cases that cannot be reasonably settled, the jury serves the important function of resolving such disputes—whether the dispute be over fault, causation, damages, or a combination of these factors.

It is clear that the item of dignitary losses drives up the cost of auto liability insurance. But added cost is not a valid objection if such damages are a necessary or proper item of recovery.

Probably the most important objection to recovery for pain and suffering damages—though the objection is generally not expressed directly—derives from a feeling that pain and suffering damages are not real, or are not bona fide.[6] Certainly such damages are not considered by no-fault proponents to be as bona fide as out-of-pocket losses, since recovery for the latter is retained while recovery for the former is dropped. This suspicious attitude toward noneconomic damages is evidenced by the early reluctance to permit recovery of damages for intentional and negligent infliction of emotional distress, where there was no accompanying physical injury (Dobbs 2000, § 302).

It is apparent that money can never adequately compensate for the pain and loss of enjoyment of life caused by personal injury. But we have long opted in favor of payment of money damages as a surrogate for the losses inflicted by tortious personal injury. As long as we choose that method of compensation, there is no satisfactory reason for excluding compensation for a central and important part of those damages, which consist of pain and suffering, mental distress, and loss of enjoyment of life.

Collateral Sources

Proponents of no-fault auto insurance also widely advocate abolition of the collateral source rule (Schermer 1995, chapters 14, 63). Under this rule one can recover from the tortfeasor as well as another source (typically a private or public insurer) for essentially the same injury. For example, a tort victim might have health or accident insurance that pays for her medical expenses incurred in an auto accident, but she would still be entitled to recover those expenses from the tortfeasor that caused the accident.

The objection to the collateral source rule is that it allows for double recovery, which is considered economically wasteful. The rule has been attacked and abrogated in whole or in part by tort retrenchment legislation (Schwartz 1997), as well as by no-fault plans.

In some situations there would be no double recovery because the victim's insurer would have a right of subrogation against the tortfeasor. In these situations, if the no-fault coverage is to receive a credit for the collateral source payment, the right of subrogation would have to be eliminated, thus making the collateral source the primary payor for the item of damages in issue and defeating internalization of that cost to the cause of the accident.

The argument in favor of retaining the collateral source rule is that the tortfeasor should not receive the benefit of the thrift of the victim, or the thrift of the victim's benefactors, whether they are gratuitous or nongratuitous. Thus, if the victim has, for example, maintained insurance privately, or in conjunction with his employer, or as a taxpayer to the government, he and not the wrongdoer should receive the benefit of that insurance.

The double-recovery argument is questionable. In the tort context, the overwhelming number of auto claims are disposed of by settlement, which is generally less than for full recovery, so the collateral source can make up for the shortfall. In no fault, a collateral source can help make up for the lack of full payment under that system. Even in the minority of cases where a no-fault or tort claim goes to judgment, that judgment may not in fact be for full recovery, especially where the claimant must pay her attorney's fee out of the judgment.

An area in which the collateral source rule remains in full force and effect is with regard to life insurance proceeds. These collateral source proceeds are never credited against a tort claim. The reason is that the deceased insured has paid for the insurance, and she—not the tortfeasor—owns and is entitled to these proceeds. The same reasoning that is applied to life insurance applies to any other collateral source.

The propriety of the collateral source rule can be illustrated by a hypothetical situation. Suppose a spelunker acquires a hard hat from another person, either by purchase or by gift. When the spelunker is exploring a cave while wearing the helmet, another explorer tortiously dislodges from above a rock that falls on the spelunker's head. The helmet saves the spelunker from any serious personal injury, but the helmet itself is destroyed. The helmet is a collateral source for which the tortfeasor should pay, whether it was purchased by the spelunker for his own protection or given to him by another for that purpose.

The collateral source rule is a rule of fairness. No economic mumbo jumbo can obscure the basic fairness of the rule.

Punitive Damages

Auto no fault does not allow for the recovery of punitive damages. It is significant, however, that almost all no-fault plans provide for the exclusion from no-fault coverage where the insured is engaged in the kind of malicious, intentional, or reckless misconduct that gives rise to an award of punitive damages (Schermer 1995, § 8.01). Once the exclusion occurs, the malfeasant can then be sued in tort for the recovery of punitive damages. Thus, the no-fault schemes recognize the propriety of punitive damages for such egregious misconduct. But the devisers of the schemes were unwilling to allow recovery of such damages under the scheme itself, which is ostensibly designed only for the compensation of out-of-pocket losses.

Punitive damages have been under strong attack by the advocates of tort retrenchment. Some jurisdictions do not permit such damages to be insured against, as a matter of public policy (*Johnson & Johnson v. Aetna Casualty & Surety Co.*, 285 N. J. Super. 575, 667 A.2d 1087 (1995)). Where such insurance is available, merit rating should be applied with vigor in the majority of jurisdictions so that the malfeasant is made to bear the greater part of the cost of his misfeasance.

The principle underlying the imposition of punitive damages is also one of fairness. Here deterrence, corrective justice, and retribution combine as strong policy underpinnings for the imposition of such damages.

❏ 5. RELATIVE COSTS

Kathleen Payne (1995, 1216) states that the major arguments support-ing adoption of auto no fault have been: (1) small auto accident claims were clogging the courts; (2) fault was too difficult to determine in many cases; and

> (3) a first-party insurance system would be more efficient than third-party insurance. The efficiency would be demonstrated by lower insurance rates and higher percentages of payout per insurance premium dollar.

The difficulty of proving fault is considered in section 2. The clogging-the-courts rationale is considered in section 6. This section considers the lower-insurance-rates issue.

It is difficult to analyze the economic efficiency of no-fault versus tort auto liability, because the types of systems—both no fault and tort—as well as cultural conditions vary from jurisdiction to jurisdiction. Moreover, it is difficult, if not impossible, to factor in larger social benefits such as, for example, savings that tort law may provide through its deterrent effect on accidents.

Chapman and Trebilcock (1992, 820–22) not surprisingly conclude that the cost of no fault depends on the stringency of the tort threshold and the amount of no-fault benefits paid. In a Rand Corporation study, Carroll, Kakalik, Pace, and Adams (1991, xvi) draw the same rather obvious conclusion, and also note that the magnitude of tort loss, claim amounts, and willingness to sue vary significantly from state to state (p. xv).

Estimates of the percentage of premium dollars returned as benefits vary widely. Joost (1999, § 3.4) cites a 1971 report stating that the tort return is forty-five to fifty cents on the dollar, and a 1988 statement by the Florida insurance commissioner who said that the personal injury portion of Florida's no-fault law "paid benefits to injured parties of around 70 cents on the insurance premium dollar." Chapman and Trebilcock (1992, 818), citing a 1985 Department of Transportation (DOT) report, state that the "average net payout ratio" (amount of premium dollar repaid in benefits) was 50.2 cents on the dollar for no-fault states and 43.2 cents for tort states.

An American Bar Association report (Epstein 1995, 1052–54) refers to a "frequently cited" DOT auto accident study, which concludes that "it costs about $1.07 in administrative expenses for each $1.00 in net benefits delivered to the accident victim" under the tort system. The report points out that under "DOT's own calculations, two-thirds of the $1.07 figure represent the insurance companies' internal administrative expense," and it says "as we shall see elsewhere in this report, those expenses might actually be higher under no-fault."

Any calculation as to the amount of benefit returned on the premium dollar, to indicate the profitability and efficiency of an insurance system, is inherently misleading because the insurance company makes money on the premium dollars collected. If, for example, each premium dollar earns 20 percent of its value, then the percentage of profitability is substantially increased.

A no-fault plan can produce substantial savings compared to tort, or it can increase costs, say O'Connell et al. (1996, 69), depending on the plan's design and variables such as the size of benefits, "the nature and extent of any barrier to tort claims," and the "litigiousness of the state's populace." They attack the medical-threshold no-fault system as being subject to manipulation to meet the threshold: "The estimated costs of excess claiming nationwide have been enormous. Padding of soft injury claims has caused medical costs to be 59% higher than they would be" (O'Connell et al. 1996, 71).

Dewees, Duff, and Trebilcock (1996, 56–57) say U.S. studies estimate "that no-fault jurisdictions exhibit substantial increases in the frequency of automobile insurance payments, particularly for income losses and victims of single-car accidents." Chapman and Trebilcock (1992, 819) state that U.S. data indicate that "on average, no-fault states have higher auto injury insurance premiums than those in pure tort states." The add-on no-fault schemes, they say, have proven to be quite costly. According to one report, "between 1971 and 1977, premium increases in add-on states were more than twice as large as those in pure tort states."

In testimony before the Senate Commerce Committee on the *Auto Choice Reform Act* (S. 625) on 9 September 1998, Mark Mandell, president of the Association of Trial Lawyers of America, said that since 1976, Nevada, Georgia, and Connecticut had repealed their no-fault laws and returned to the tort system. "The year after Georgia repealed its law," he testified, auto insurance rates in that state dropped 6 percent while premiums in no-fault states increased by 7 percent. "Likewise," he said, "the year after Connecticut repealed no-fault, its rates dropped 7 percent" (U.S. Senate 1998).

In testimony before the House Commerce Committee on the *Auto Choice Reform Act of 1997* (H.R. 2021), Harvey Rosenfield stated:

> No-fault states have the highest average automobile insurance premiums. Of the ten states where auto insurance was the most expensive in 1989, eight were no-fault states. . . . In 1995, six of the top ten most expensive states (including D.C.) had no-fault systems. . . . [I]n 1995, New York—the model state for the "verbal threshold" no-fault proposals promoted by the insurance industry earlier in this decade—was the fifth most expensive state in the nation (U.S. House 1998).

In a law review article, Rosenfield (1998, 69) catalogs in detail the data he gave in testimony before the House Committee. He states that 1995 data furnished by the National Association of Insurance Commissioners "demonstrate that no-fault systems—including mandatory no-fault laws—are more expensive than personal responsibility systems based on tort liability." He quotes from the 1992 no-fault press manual of the "nation's largest auto insurance company," State Farm:

> The adoption of no-fault reparation systems may or may not lead to a reduction in the cost of auto insurance. The advantage of no-fault lies in a redistribution of insurance benefits based on need rather than fault, not its potential cost saving (pp. 94–95).

Quoting a 1990 study of auto accident litigation in Michigan, Rosenfield (p. 100) said the study "determined that 22% (241) of the 1119 reported cases concerned the bodily injury threshold requirement, where the question was whether the claimant's injuries were serious enough to permit a suit against a negligent third party."

The auto-tort system does not appear to be creating a runaway litigation problem, either in terms of the number of suits or the amount of awards. Chapman and Trebilcock (1992, 816) found that in California in 1977, one-half of all auto liability claims involved payments of less than $1,000, "and only 11% were for $5,000 or more." Nonpecuniary damages (pain and suffering and the like) constitute a substantial portion of U.S. auto-tort payments: "Over 60% of U.S. auto liability payments relate to non-pecuniary damages."

According to the Bureau of Justice Statistics, 31.9 percent of the civil cases disposed of in 1996 in the state courts in the nation's seventy-five largest counties were auto-tort cases. The median award for such cases was $18,000 (DeFrances and Litras 1999). In federal courts for 1996–97, the percentage of auto-tort cases was 19.4 percent and the median award was $91,000 (Litras and DeFrances 1999).

The number of accidents and deaths on U.S. highways is decreasing. Drawing on National Safety Council statistics, Schwartz (1994, 393) notes that in 1972, a total of "56,278 Americans were killed in highway accidents," while in 1992 this number had decreased to 40,300. "The decrease in fatalities is even more dramatic," Schwartz says, "if fatalities are calculated as a percentage of population or as a percentage of miles driven."[7] What role tort law has played in this decline, he says, is unclear. "Important causes certainly include federal regulation of vehicle design, state laws requiring safety belt use, increased public law sanctions for drunk driving, and changing public attitudes towards both drunk driving and safety belts."

The insurance industry is not suffering a financial decline. The Underwriters' Wire service (1999, 1) reported that the "U.S. property/casualty insurance industry's consolidated net income after tax rose to a record $35.6 billion in 1997, a 45.7 percent increase from $24.4 billion in 1996." In an article titled "Insurance," the *Houston Chronicle* reported on 2 June 1998 that "insurance costs escalated 150 percent in the 1980s in spite of declining accident rates." The *San Diego Union-Tribune* reported on 4 July 1999 that for the "first time in 26 years, the price of auto insurance has dropped," according to the Insurance Information Institute. The Institute attributed the drop to heightened competition among insurers, safer driving by baby boomers, lower new car prices, less public tolerance of drunk driving, and greater regulation by insurers and states of fraudulent claims.

The effort to decrease auto insurance costs by substituting no fault for tort liability is reminiscent of the tort retrenchment period of the 1980s. Opponents of tort law in general maintained that tort claims and insurance rates could be dramatically reduced by the passage of statutes retrenching on tort remedies. Such statutes were widely passed by the states. In a careful study of insurance rate and loss cost (expected claims cost) movement in every state from 1985 through 1998, Robert Hunter and Joanne Doroshow (1999, 2) found that

> tort law limits enacted since the liability insurance crisis of the mid-1980s have not lowered insurance rates in the ensuing years. States with little or no tort law restrictions have experienced the same level of insurance rates as those states that enacted severe restrictions on victims' rights.

They concluded that the "liability insurance crisis" of the mid-1980s was "ultimately found to be caused not by legal system excesses but by the economic cycle of the insurance industry."

Rosenfield attributes much of the cause of high automobile insurance rates not to tort litigation, but to lack of adequate state regulation of the insurance industry, and to the industry's own unwillingness to adequately regulate itself (Rosenfield 1998, 103–19). A 1988 ballot initiative, Proposition 103, adopted in California, required auto and other property casualty insurance rates to be rolled back by 20 percent (p. 102). As a result of this rollback, between 1989 and 1997 "insurance companies operating in California issued over $1.18 billion in premium refunds to more than seven million policyholders" (p. 104). The rollback formula capped the insurers' rate of return; prohibited insurance companies from engaging in bookkeeping practices "that inflate their claims losses"; limited the amount insurers can set aside as surplus and reserves; and forbade insurers "from passing through to consumers the costs of the industry's lobbying, political contributions, institutional advertising, the unsuccessful defense of discrimination cases, bad faith damage awards, and fines or penalties" (p. 104).

Proposition 103 effected a number of other insurance reforms. It "repealed the insurance industry's exemption from the antitrust laws and prohibited the operation of 'rating' and 'advisory' organizations set up by the industry to circulate pricing and policy information to insurance companies" (Rosenfield 1998, 106–07). It repealed the state's antirebate law, which prohibited brokers from reducing their commissions in order to offer consumers a lower price (p. 107). It "repealed the statutory prohibition on the sale of insurance by financial institutions," "empowered consumers to more easily negotiate group insurance purchases" (p. 108), and required the insurance commissioner "to provide consumers with a current rate comparison survey for automobile, homeowner, and other lines of insurance" (p. 109).

Proposition 103 prohibited the use of a "territorial rating" system for determining auto insurance premiums. Under this system premiums were determined "by calculating claims payments made within the motorist's zip code" (Rosenfield 1998, 109). Rosenfield (p. 110) continues:

A 1986 study prepared for the California Assembly by the National Insurance Consumers Organization (NICO) illustrates the discriminatory impact of the much criticized zip code-based system of territorial rating. Of the 4.9 million cars insured in California between 1982 and 1984, 95.4% had no claims. In central Los Angeles, 93.5% of the cars avoided claims. The modest difference in the number of claims is to be expected, given population density and reliance on automobiles in Los Angeles. Nevertheless, accident-free Los Angeles drivers paid on the average 66% more for property damage liability insurance than did the average *accident-free* driver outside Los Angeles [emphasis in original].

Instead of the zip code system, Proposition 103 required auto insurance premiums to be based "primarily upon three rating factors in decreasing order of importance: a motorist's driving safety record, the number of miles he or she drives each year, and the motorist's years of driving experience" (Rosenfield 1998, 109). The measure further required insurers "to grant a 20% good-driver discount to all qualifying consumers: individuals with a virtually clean driving record (one moving violation is permitted) for the preceding three years" (p. 110).

"The failure of insurers to service particular communities," Rosenfield (1998, 111) said, "particularly in urban areas, has been amply documented." Proposition 103 "specifies that any good driver, as defined in the initiative, has the right to purchase an auto insurance policy from the insurer of his or her choice" (p. 112).

A frequent complaint against auto insurers, says Rosenfield (1998, 112), is that they "may cancel or fail to renew policies without justification, sometimes merely for the act of filing a claim." Proposition 103 prohibits cancellation or failure to renew "unless based on one of three specific reasons: nonpayment of premium, fraud, or the policyholder presents a substantial increase in the hazard insured against."

In an attempt to head off adoption of Proposition 103, the insurance industry sponsored Proposition 104, which would have adopted a no-fault auto insurance system with a verbal threshold modeled on that of New York. "To pass Proposition 104 and defeat Proposition 103," Rosenfield (1998, 83–84) says, "insurers spent over sixty million dollars." Proposition 104 "was defeated by a three-to-one margin," while 103 "was approved by 51% of the voters."

Rosenfield (1998, 84–86) concludes that auto liability insurance costs are much more a function of predatory insurance practices than they are a choice between tort and no fault:

> The passage of Proposition 103 represented a dramatic turning point in the insurance reform debate. Driven by the California initiative, insurance industry reform occupied the focus of policymakers throughout the United States. . . .
>
> The insurance industry's initial response was stunned, then angry, denial. Determined to discourage the similar efforts underway in other states, various insurers filed nearly 100 legal challenges to Proposition 103; none succeeded. Meanwhile, Proposition 103's passage inspired similar efforts in nearly every state legislature in the nation. Despite the industry's efforts to blunt further Proposition 103-style reforms, 19 states enacted insurance industry reforms. . . .
>
> By contrast, the industry's intensive promotion of no-fault as an alternative to insurance industry reform has been a complete failure. Industry-sponsored no-fault legislation was defeated in high profile battles in several states. A "pure" no-fault ballot measure, one of a package of three tort "reform" measures sponsored by the business community, including insurance companies, was placed before California voters in March, 1996; it was rejected by 65% of voters despite a $19 million campaign in its favor. Indeed, since 1988, there have been serious efforts to repeal no-fault laws in at least six states; three were successful.

❑ 6. EXPEDITIOUSNESS

> Whether 'tis nobler in the mind to suffer
> The slings and arrows of outrageous fortune,
> Or to take arms against a sea of troubles. . . .
> For who would bear the whips and scorns of time,
> Th' oppressor's wrong, the proud man's contumely,
> The pangs of despis'd love, the law's delay,
> The insolence of office, and the spurns
> That patient merit of th' unworthy takes,
> —*Hamlet*, Act III, Sc. 1, by William Shakespeare

Hamlet's choice was either to bear the law's delay and so on, or, by the adoption of a new (no-fault?) plan, to encounter the unknown—which might be worse than the known. We have more knowledge of the effect of the choice between no-fault and tort, and the effect of the law's delay, and even of the insolence of office, than Hamlet did in choosing between life and that "bourn" from which no traveler returns.

Court Clogging

In *Pinnick v. Cleary* (360 Mass. 1, 271 N. E. 2d 592, n. 13 (1971)), the Massachusetts Supreme Court upheld the constitutionality of that state's no-fault auto insurance law, in large part on the grounds that the law was intended to relieve the clogging of the courts, which allegedly resulted from the filing of small bodily injury auto claims. The court found that in the mid- and late 1950s approximately two-thirds of the cases filed in the superior court of that state consisted of such claims, and of those claims approximately 80 percent of the ones resulting in a verdict for the plaintiff were for an amount of less than $200. It is unclear from the opinion whether those verdicts were for personal injury or property damage, since they were simply described as "claims for small amounts."

These figures should be compared with more recent data, considered in the previous section. The Bureau of Justice Statistics found that in 1996 about one-third of the cases disposed of in the state courts of the nation's seventy-five largest counties were auto-tort cases (DeFrances and Litras 1999), and that about one-fifth of the cases disposed of in the federal district courts for 1996–97 were auto-tort cases (Litras and DeFrances 1999). These numbers hardly dominated the courts. The median auto accident award in these respective forums was $18,000 and $91,000. These can hardly be considered small claims.

The evidence of court clogging with small auto personal injury claims is not convincing. Moreover, it must be borne in mind that auto property damage claims are not removed from the judicial system by any of the U.S. no-fault plans, although these claims may be relatively small in amount and large in number. In *Basic Protection* (1965, 367), Keeton and O'Connell advocated exclusion of auto property claims from the no-fault system, on the grounds that these claims were likely to be readily settled in most cases. But it must be borne in mind, as noted in section 4 on compensation, that something on the order of 98 percent of personal injury claims are settled, so automobile personal injury claims do not appear statistically to be more difficult to settle than automobile property damage claims.

Richard Epstein (2000, 1010) notes that "in 1989 for each 100 property damage claims [in California] there were 56 claims for bodily injury." It is unclear whether the claims he is referring to are exclusively related to automobile accidents, but the statement indicates that property claims are clearly not an insignificant portion of tort litigation.

The court-clogging issue is not persuasive. There are, for example, approximately as many contract as tort cases disposed of in the state courts (Ostrom and Kander 1998, 35), yet no one complains of court clogging from contract cases. The size of the case, in terms of dollar amount claimed, should not be determinative of the issue of court clogging, since the importance of rendering justice does not depend on the number of dollars involved. If the courts are inadequate to mete out justice, the solution is to create more courts rather than to reduce or ration justice.

The real issue is one of delay. Is the auto-tort system unduly slow, as compared to no fault? Justice delayed can amount to justice denied.

Time to Payment

The Bureau of Justice Statistics shows that for 1996 the median time from filing to verdict in state automobile jury cases in the seventy-five largest counties of the nation was 19.2 months (DeFrances and Litras 1999). The median time from filing to termination of such cases in the federal district courts for 1996–97 was 15.2 months (Litras and DeFrances 1999).

Chapman and Trebilcock (1992, 818) provide the experience for payment of auto claims, apparently by settlement, for tort and no fault in Quebec for 1978. Their statistics show 35 percent of the tort cases settling in less than six months, and 96 percent of the no-fault cases settling within the same period of time.

In all likelihood small claims settle expeditiously because the stakes are not high. Chapman and Trebilcock (1992, 817) indicate as much when they say that "both U.S. and Canadian studies disclose considerable delays in the payment of third-party benefits, particularly to claimants with serious injuries involving higher pecuniary losses and a greater likelihood of litigation and attorney involvement." The median auto liability awards given above in the Bureau of Justice Statistics report indicate that the amounts litigated in both state and federal courts were large.

The length of time between claims and payment—either by settlement or by judicial disposition—is probably not as critical for the tort victim as is the need for resources after the injury has occurred. There are medical and other bills to be paid by a victim, who may be disabled and unable to work. Lack of resources may also place the accident victim in an unfavorable bargaining position with the tortfeasor, who may be able to force a one-sided settlement on the victim owing to the latter's economic exigencies. As Dewees, Duff, and Trebilcock (1996, 22–27) find, however, many persons will have assets available to meet an emergency situation created by an auto accident:

> In both the United States and Canada, first-party compensation for the losses associated with automobile injuries is available from various sources. In 1985, 85% of American families held at least some life insurance, although on average this amounted to less than 26 months of disposable personal income per family (less than the life insurance industry's rule of thumb of 4–5 years). Similarly, almost 85% of Americans are protected by one or more forms of private health insurance, and Medicare and Medicaid programs exist to meet the urgent needs of many of the remainder. In addition, motorists in tort states can purchase first-party "medical payments" insurance, covering medical expenses for purely auto-related injuries, while those in no-fault jurisdictions are entitled to medical and rehabilitation expense benefits of varying amounts, depending on the particular scheme. In Canada, public health insurance pays for virtually all medical and physical rehabilitation expenses. . . .
>
> . . . Although private insurers sell Medical Payments insurance for purely auto-related injuries, insurers in tort jurisdictions have been unwilling to offer income interruption coverage as well. Private long-term disability protection generally replaces 60%–70% of income, but it is held by only about 20% of U.S. employees and 40% of full-time employees in Ontario. Employment-related short-term disability income protection and sick leave are more widely held (by about 56% of American employees, according to 1984 data), but they pay benefits for only a short duration.

American jurisdictions that have threshold and add-on, no-fault auto liability coverages may provide the auto accident victim with a source of tide-over income that will support her until she can collect a tort claim arising out of the accident. This eventuality arises from the proposition that no-fault benefits are likely to be paid promptly, because the amount owing can be readily determined and can be paid in installments as the sums come due.

In *Basic Protection* (1965, 152), Keeton and O'Connell recognize this possibility of claims financing in criticizing the 1965 proposal made by the California State Bar for a compulsory form of loss insurance. They respond:

"Indeed one might expect the loss insurance benefits to be used often to finance tort suits." They imply the same reservations in criticizing Blum and Kalven's proposal for "making social security payments to all victims but allowing victims of tortfeasors to sue in tort with a deduction of the social welfare benefits from tort recovery" (p. 233). They scoff at this proposal, saying: "Here again one can scarcely be sanguine about the attitude of the insurance companies to their partial displacement, given their morbid fear of even compulsory tort liability insurance as a governmental 'foot in the door'" (pp. 233–34). Earlier, they support compulsory liability insurance against the charge that it may increase litigation by raising the expectations of automobile accident victims: "First, increased claims consciousness in itself is not necessarily a regrettable trend. If losses have been suffered, why shouldn't claims be made?" (p. 99) And, if rightful claims should be made, what is wrong with providing an economic mechanism by which those claims can be practicably asserted?

There is a striking parallel between workers' compensation benefits and no-fault benefits as a means of financing justifiable tort litigation. Peter Bell and Jeffrey O'Connell (1997, 208) note that third-party workplace tort claims have been used as a corrective measure to compensate for workers' compensation payment inadequacies. The same can be true for no-fault payments. Both no-fault and workers' compensation payments may be inadequate, but they provide a powerful means of tiding over the claimant financially when she needs to assert a tort claim.

A few jurisdictions have recognized the propriety of allowing an attorney to underwrite a claimant's living expenses as a means of weathering the financial hardship of pursuing a claim (*Louisiana State Bar Association v. Edwins*, 329 So. 2d 437 (La. 1976)). This proposition has not been widely adopted, but it has much merit. If a claim is justifiable, then it seems equally justifiable to provide the legal means for waiting out the claim, where an expeditious termination is not forthcoming.

❏ 7. THE BEST SYSTEM
Add-On No Fault

In many respects the best system for auto accident coverage would be the add-on system that is now in effect in eight states (Dewees, Duff, and Trebilcock 1996). This system provides a minimum no-fault coverage for medical expenses and lost earnings, with immediate entry (no threshold barrier) into the tort system.

If such a system were chosen, several policy decisions would have to be made. Would the add-on be optional or mandatory? If a tort claim were available (i.e., if the other driver were at fault), would any add-on payments be credited against any tort recovery, or would such payments be treated as a collateral source? If the collateral source approach were taken, it should be determined whether or not the add-on insurer should have a right of subrogation against the tortfeasor for any add-on payments made to the insured.

Several studies indicate that the add-on system is very expensive (Bell and O'Connell 1997, 211; Rosenfield 1998, 87; Chapman and Trebilcock 1992, 819). The expense perhaps cuts in favor of the add-on choice being made optional. On the other hand, protection of the public welfare by the provision of basic accident support argues in favor of a compulsory system and is one of the primary appeals of no-fault insurance. Higher insurance prices may reduce the number of automobiles on the highways—a desideratum from an environmental perspective. But against this advantage must be weighed the need for access of lower-income groups to a mode of transportation—particularly where moderately priced public transportation is not readily available.

The argument for treating add-on payments as a collateral source—with or without insurer subrogation—is supported by the economic argument of cost internalization. That is, if the tortfeasor has caused x amount of damage to the victim, that loss should be placed on the tortfeasor rather than the victim or her insurer in order to more effectively internalize the costs of the accident to the tortfeasor.

An argument against subrogation is that nonsubrogation may allow the victim to be made more nearly whole. This argument is countered by the assertion that relatively small claims are overcompensated in tort, but as considered previously, the claim of overcompensation may not be valid. Everyone seems to agree that larger claims are typically undercompensated, thus arguing against subrogation for such claims. The presence or absence of subrogation may, however, have a significant effect on the cost of add-on insurance.

If individuals are adequately covered by non–auto health and unemployment insurance, then add-on coverage may be superfluous and such superfluity argues in favor of add-on being made noncompulsory.

If the happy day ever arrives when universal health insurance is made available from public or private sources under the auspices of the federal government, the need for add-on auto insurance will be substantially reduced. Its need as a basic support component may then be limited to income replacement.

Threshold No Fault

The most common form of no-fault auto coverage in the United States is threshold no fault. Twelve states have made such coverage mandatory, and three have made it optional (Dewees, Duff, and Trebilcock 1996, 22). The threshold may be defined in terms of dollars (medical expenses incurred) or seriousness of injury (the verbal threshold, described as permanent injury, serious disfigurement, death, and the like). Until the injuries reach the threshold, the victim cannot sue in tort. Once the threshold is reached, the victim can sue in tort for injuries suffered. The same questions of collateral source and subrogation previously considered are raised here. The optional version of threshold no fault raises some of the same issues presented by the proposed federal optional system, considered below.

The threshold system has resulted in extensive claims pressure to overcome the threshold, and this pressure is particularly evident where the threshold is defined in terms of medical expenses incurred. Insofar as the expenses are manufactured or trumped up, the dollar threshold presents a distinctly undesirable social consequence. But of course in many cases the expenses are fully justified. The verbal threshold presents difficulties in defining seriousness of injury sufficient to justify meeting the threshold.

The threshold system has the unfortunate consequence of removing the tort remedy, including recovery for noneconomic damages, in a large number of cases. The justification for doing so is dubious. The court-clogging argument, considered in the previous section, is unpersuasive, as is the overcompensation argument. It has always been difficult to explain—other than on grounds of political expediency—why claims above the threshold can be brought in tort while those below cannot.

Pure No Fault

No U.S. jurisdiction has adopted pure no fault—that is, a system whereby no-fault liability is substituted entirely for auto-tort liability. The reasons for the retention of tort—either with add-on, or above a threshold—may be manifold. Whatever those reasons are, it seems clear that as a political matter tort cannot be eliminated from the U.S. auto arena. Indeed, Keeton and O'Connell (1965), the most notable proponents of no fault in this country, proposed only a threshold system. The retention of auto-tort liability in this country, in whole or in part, indicates that tort law, in conjunction with complementary public and private sources, is satisfactorily serving its compensatory function—or at least, that no fault is not seen in the United States as a desirable substitute to serve that function. No fault serves few if any deterrent and corrective justice functions, while automobile tort liability serves both these functions.

Elective No Fault

In 1999, identical bills were introduced in the Senate (S. 837) and the House (H.R. 1475) to enable each state at its option either to choose a no-fault auto system, or to retain its present tort or mixed tort-no-fault system. First, each state must opt in or out of the system. If it opts out, then the state retains it present system. If it opts in, then each car owner in the state must decide whether to be covered by no fault or to remain in the tort system. Thus far, the bills have not been adopted by either House or Senate.

A number of attempts have been made in the past to adopt a federal mandatory, no-fault system, binding on all the states, but all such attempts have failed (Nolan and Ursin 1995, chapter 8).

It is unclear why the federal proponents of no fault think the elective proposal would be any more likely to pass than a mandatory proposal. Perhaps they think that some mystique associated with state choice will give the bill a better chance of passage.

It is also unclear why these proponents think a federal elective bill serves any purpose, since each state is already free to adopt its own no-fault system. Perhaps they think that the cachet of a federal elective bill will cause states to approve the proposal. Perhaps they think that some states will adopt the bill by inertia, because section 10 of the bill requires an affirmative finding against adoption, either by the insurance commissioner or by the legislature of each state, in order to forestall the federal law from going into effect in that state.[8]

The bill raises constitutional questions. Congress may not have the power under the commerce clause to adopt the bill (*United States v. Morrison*, 120 S. Ct. 1740 (2000); Phillips 1997). Even if Congress does have such power, the bill may be an unconstitutional infringement on states' rights under the tenth amendment (*New York v. United States*, 505 U. S. 144 (1992); LeBow 1997).

If a car owner in an electing state were to choose to remain in the tort system, he could sue in tort any other car owner in the state who made a similar choice and recover his tort damages (H.R. 1475 1999, S. 837 1999). Two owners electing no fault who are involved in an accident may recover their economic losses, without regard to fault, from their own insurers (H.R. 1475 1999, § 8(9); S. 837 1999, § 8(a)).

If a no-fault election and a tort election car owner are involved in an accident, the no-fault owner recovers his no-fault benefits (H.R. 1475 1999, § 8(b)(1); S. 837 1999, § 8(b)(1)). The tort-election owner can collect nothing unless the no-fault owner is at fault, in which event the tort-election owner can collect from the no-fault election owner only for his "uncompensated economic loss (and not for noneconomic loss)" (H.R. 1475 1999, § 8(a)(1)(A); S. 837 1999 § 8(a)(1)(A)). The tort-election owner may also recover from his uninsured or underinsured motorist (UM) insurer for any excess liability where the other party is at fault (H.R. 1475 1999, § 7(b); S. 837 1999, § 7(b)).

A no-fault election owner may recover from another such owner who is at fault, or from a tort-election owner who is at fault, for any "uncompensated economic loss (and not for noneconomic loss)" that he may have suffered (H.R. 1475 1999, § 8(b)(2); S. 837 1999, § 8(b)(2)).

Apparently, the collateral source rule would be abolished for all claims under the bill, and a claimant could only recover his permissible damages minus collateral sources (H.R. 1475 1999, § 6(b)(1)(B), 8(j)(2); S. 837 1999, §§ 6(b)(1)(B), 8(j)(2)).

It is unclear how the federal election bill, if enacted by Congress and adopted by a state, would play out in practice in that state. Some believe that the high-risk car owners would elect the no-fault option, since that would expose them to less liability and presumably to lower insurance premiums (Chapman and Trebilcock 1992, 825). There would be little incentive for the would-be tort elector to remain in tort, since she could never collect her collateral sources in addition to any tort or no-fault recovery, and could never collect her noneconomic loss except against another tort elector, or under her own UM coverage where an at-fault, no-fault elector was involved. Thus the no-fault elector would shift much of the risk of loss from himself to the tort elector. Some also believe that the tort electors would end up paying for the fault of the no-fault electors, either through higher premiums for their UM coverage or through insurer shifting of fault responsibility from no-fault to tort electors by means of premium setting (Senate Committee on Commerce, Science, and Transportation 1998). The end result might then be that the choice system would effectively deprive the tort elector of any real choice.

The Tort System

The tort system presents all the advantages heretofore considered, and on balance seems clearly preferable over any no-fault substitute system. In order to make the tort system fully effective, the collateral source rule should be retained and the tort remedy should be untrammeled by statutory restrictions such as caps on recoverable damages and the like. The comparative fault rule—which is the overwhelming majority rule in the United States—abolishes the harshness of the old common-law tort rule of contributory negligence as a total bar, and adjusts the liabilities between plaintiff and defendant more fairly.

The dual goals of automobile tort law are to compensate the injured and to deter those at fault. The compensatory role may be aided by other public and private sources of compensation. Likewise, the deterrent role may be aided by many other sources. Not the least among these other sources are more stringent statutory penalties for speeding and drunken driving; better automobile and highway safety design; and regular, required auto safety inspections. Automobile use should be discouraged both for safety and environmental reasons, and public transportation should be encouraged and facilitated for these reasons. The United States made a tragic choice when it opted for widespread automobile transportation in lieu of widespread passenger train transportation.

A sine qua non for effective auto-tort compensation and deterrence is that the car owner should be required to carry compulsory automobile liability insurance in reasonable amounts. Such a requirement can surely be enforced, if its importance is given proper recognition.

NOTES

1. For a capsule summary of auto no-fault plans, see Schermer (1995), chapters 14 and 63. Subrogation is widely allowed by a no-fault insurer when the insured has a third-party tort claim (Schermer 1995, §§ 19.01, 19.05).

Under Keeton and O'Connell's (1965, 278, 400–401) no-fault proposal, nongratuitous collateral sources (with the exception of life insurance) are deducted from any no-fault recovery.

The proposed federal choice law, H.R. 1475 and S. 837, introduced in Congress in 1999, provides in section 6(b)(1)(B) for the deduction of workers' compensation and disability insurance collateral sources. Section 8(j)(2) permits collateral subrogation and otherwise abolishes the collateral source rule (S. 837, 1999, 106th Cong., 1st sess.; H.R. 1475, 1999, 106th Cong., 1st sess.).

2. On the other hand, a growing number of cases indicate the danger of air bags (e.g., premature deployment). See *Perez-Trujillo v. Volvo Car Corp.*, 137 F.3d 50 (1st Cir. 1998).

3. Legal and behavioral commentators have concluded "that the certainty of punishment has a far more significant impact on deterrence than the severity of the penalty" (*G. J. D. v. Johnson*, 713 A.2d 1127 (Pa. 1998)). The high rate of auto-tort settlement indicates that defendant's perception of liability is high—although the expectation of accident involvement may be low.

4. Leslie Yalof Garfield (1998) notes a recent study which indicates that "drivers who talk on car phones are thirty-four times more likely to have an accident than drivers who do not use car phones," and she suggests that such use should be criminalized.

5. In their seminal work on no-fault auto insurance (1965, 264–65), Keeton and O'Connell recognize the propriety of insurance merit rating based on fault determination, which can be retained for serious tort injuries above the no-fault threshold. On the other hand, they have "serious doubts about the validity and evenhandedness of the determinations of negligence in motoring cases," and they doubt that the administrative costs of merit rating based on fault are worth the candle in "smaller cases." However, at another point they state that even under a no-fault system, insurance premium rating could be based on the number of the insured's involvements in accidents. While recognizing "that luck to some extent determines whether a driver is involved in accidents," they nevertheless conclude that such involvement "has considerable correlation with bad driving habits, and thus one might use rating categories based on involvement to give weight in a general way to fault and deterrence at small administrative cost" (pp. 255–56).

The proposed federal choice law, S. 837 and H.R. 1475, introduced in Congress in 1999, provides in section 8(n)-(o) that neither tort liability nor no-fault premiums may be increased (or a policy cancelled or not renewed) based on involvement in an accident, unless fault can be ascribed to the insured as a result of such involvement.

Under the CAL. INS. CODE § 1861.02 (1993), an insured motorist is entitled to a 20-percent premium discount below what she would otherwise be required to pay if, among other things, she has not during the preceding three years been involved in an auto-accident-causing property damage where she was principally at fault. See § 1861.025 (1999).

While a true merit or experience rating should allow premium rate increases based only on accidents that result from the insured's fault, many liability insurers probably increase individual premiums based merely on accident involvement of the insured, without regard to whether the insured was at fault, in order to achieve administrative efficiency along the lines discussed by Keeton and O'Connell (1965). Moreover, if an insured disputed fault, a lawsuit might prove necessary to resolve the dispute.

6. J. David Cassidy (2000) compared auto whiplash claims filed in Saskatch-ewan six months before and one year after that province adopted no-fault auto liability insurance in 1995. Cassidy found a drop of about one-quarter in the number of such claims, and a drop of about one-half in the time from injury to "closure" of such claims, before and after the adoption of no fault. He concludes: "The elimination of compensation for pain and suffering [by the adoption of no fault] is associated with a decreased incidence and improved prognosis of whiplash injury" (p. 1179). This study appears to suggest that pain and suffering vanished when the basis for recovery disappeared.

The Saskatchewan study may be severely flawed, among other reasons, because—as one critic points out—health-care providers under the Saskatchewan no-fault plan, as a policy matter, cease treating whiplash claims twelve weeks after injury (Middleton 2000, 5). "Closure" occurs, in other words, not because the pain has stopped, but because payments are stopped.

7. Compare this with the statement by Robert Pear (1999) asserting that the National Academy of Sciences had recently called for a new federal agency to protect medical patients, because the number killed each year by medical malpractice is "44,000 to 98,000, numbers that exceed those who die from highway accidents and breast cancer."

8. In the *Auto Choice Reform Act of 1999* (S. 837 and H.R. 1475), Section 10, Applicability to States, provides:

(a) ELECTION OF NONAPPLICABILITY BY STATES—Subject to subsections (c) through (e), this Act shall apply with respect to a State, unless –

(1) by not later than the earlier of the date that is 1 year after the date of enactment of this Act or the expiration of the first regular legislative session of the State beginning after the date of enactment of this Act, the State enacts a statute that –

(A) cites the authority of this subsection;

(B) declares the election of that State that this Act shall not apply with respect to that State; and

(C) contains no other provision; or

(2)(A) the State official charged with jurisdiction over insurance rates for motor vehicles makes a finding that this Act does not apply by reasons of the applicability of the conditions described in subsection (b)(1)(A); and

(B) that finding is made and any review described in subsection (b)(1)(B) is completed not later than the date specified in subsection (b)(1)(C).

(b) NONAPPLICABILITY BASED ON STATE FINDING –

(1) IN GENERAL—This Act shall not apply with respect to a State, if –

(A) the State official charged with jurisdiction over insurance rates for motor vehicles makes a finding that the statewide average motor vehicle premiums for bodily injury insurance in effect immediately before the date of enactment of this Act will not be reduced by an average of at least 30 percent for persons choosing the personal injury protection system, in the amounts required under section 6 (without including in the calculation for personal injury protection insureds any costs for uninsured, underinsured, or medical payments coverage);

(B) the finding described under subparagraph (A) is supported by evidence adduced in a public hearing and reviewable under the applicable State administrative procedure law; and

(C) the finding described under subparagraph (A) is made, and any review of such finding under subparagraph (B) is completed, not later than 120 days after the date of enactment of this Act.

(2) COMPARISON OF BODILY INJURY PREMIUMS—For purposes of making a comparison under paragraph (1)(A) of premiums for personal injury protection with preexisting premiums for bodily injury insurance (in effect immediately before the date of enactment of this Act), the preexisting bodily injury insurance premiums shall include premiums for –

(A) bodily injury liability, uninsured and underinsured motorists' liability, and medical payments coverage; and

(B) if applicable, no-fault benefits under a no-fault motor vehicle law or add-on law.

(c) IMPLEMENTATION PERIOD—Except as provided in subsection (d), if a State fails to enact a law by the applicable date specified in paragraph (1) of subsection (a) or if a finding described in paragraph (2) of that subsection is not made and reviewed by the date specified in subsection (b)(1)(C), this Act shall apply to that State beginning on the date that is 270 days after the later of those dates.

(d) ACCELERATED APPLICABILITY –

(1) IN GENERAL—Subject to paragraph (2), a State may enact a law that provides for the implementation of the provisions of this Act in that State before an otherwise applicable date determined under subsection (a).

(2) APPLICABILITY—If a State makes an election under paragraph (1), this Act shall apply to that State beginning on the date that is 270 days after such election.

(e) ELECTION OF NONAPPLICABILITY BY A STATE AFTER THIS ACT BECOMES APPLICABLE WITH RESPECT TO THE STATE—After this Act becomes applicable with respect to a State under subsection (c) or (d), this Act shall cease to apply with respect to that State if the State enacts a statute that meets the requirements of subparagraphs (A) through (C) of subsection (a)(1).

REFERENCES

American Law Institute. 1991. *Enterprise Responsibility for Personal Injury: Reporter's Study.* Vol. 2. Philadelphia: American Law Institute.

Auto Choice Reform Act of 1999, 106th Cong., 1st sess., S. 837.

Auto Choice Reform Act of 1999, 106th Cong., 1st sess., H.R. 1475.

Bell, P. A., and J. O'Connell. 1997. *Accidental Justice: The Dilemmas of Tort Law.* New Haven, Conn.: Yale University Press.

Blum, W. J., and H. Kalven, Jr. 1965. *Public Law Perspectives on a Private Law Problem: Auto Compensation Plans.* Boston: Little, Brown.

———. 1967. "The Empty Cabinet of Dr. Calabresi: Auto Accidents and General Deterrence." *University of Chicago Law Review* 34: 254–73.

Bruce, C. J. 1984. "The Deterrent Effects of Automobile Insurance and Tort Law." *Law and Policy* 6: 67–100.

Carroll, S. J., J. S. Kakalik, N. M. Pace, and J. L. Adams. 1991. *No-Fault Approaches to Compensating People Injured in Automobile Accidents*. Santa Monica, Calif.: Rand Corporation.

Cassidy, J. D. 2000. "Effect of Eliminating Compensation for Pain and Suffering on the Outcome of Insurance Claims for Whiplash Injury." *New England Journal of Medicine* 342: 1179–86.

Chapman, B., and M. J. Trebilcock. 1992. "Making Hard Choices: Lessons from the Auto Accident Compensation Debate." *Rutgers Law Review* 44: 797–869.

DeFrances, C. J., and M. F. X. Litras. 1999. *Civil Trial Cases and Verdicts in Large Counties, 1996*. Washington, D.C.: U.S. Department of Justice, Office of Justice Programs, Bureau of Justice Statistics.

Dewees, D., D. Duff, and M. Trebilcock. 1996. *Exploring the Domain of Accident Law: Taking the Facts Seriously*. New York: Oxford University Press.

Dobbs, D. B. 2000. *The Law of Torts*. St. Paul, Minn.: West Group.

Dunlop, B. 1975. "No-Fault Automobile Insurance and the Negligence Action: An Expensive Anomaly." *Osgoode Hall Law Journal* 13: 439–47.

Epstein, R. 1995. *Cases and Materials on Torts*. 6th ed. New York: Little, Brown.

———. 2000. *Cases and Materials on Torts*. 7th ed. Gaithersburg, Md.: Aspen Law and Business.

Garfield, L. Y. 1998. "A More Principled Approach to Criminalizing Negligence: A Prescription for the Legislature." *Tennessee Law Review* 65: 875–924.

Gifford, L. S., C. J. DeFrances, and M. F. X. Litras. 2000. *Civil Justice Survey of State Courts, 1996*. Washington, D.C.: U.S. Department of Justice, Office of Justice Programs, Bureau of Justice Statistics.

Green, L. 1958. *Traffic Victims: Tort Law and Insurance*. Evanston, Ill.: Northwestern University Press.

Hand, L. 1926. "The Deficiencies of Trials to Reach the Heart of the Matter." In *Lectures on Legal Topics, 1921–1922*, by J. N. Rosenberg et al. New York: Macmillan.

Harper, F., F. James, and O. Gray. 1986. *The Law of Torts*. Boston: Little, Brown.

Hubbard, F. P. 1998. "Taxing Compensatory Tort Damages for Mental Distress." *Trial* (October): 50–56.

Hunter, J. R., and J. Doroshow. 1999. *Premium Deceit: The Failure of "Tort Reform" to Cut Insurance Prices*. New York: Citizens for Corporate Accountability and Individual Rights.

Ison, T. G. 1967. *The Forensic Lottery: A Critique on Tort Liability as a System of Personal Injury Litigation*. London: Staples Press.

Joost, R. H. 1992 and 1999 supplement. 2d ed. *Automobile Insurance and No-Fault Law*. Deerfield, Ill.: Clark, Boardman, Callaghan.

Keeton, R. E., and J. O'Connell. 1965. *Basic Protection for the Traffic Victim: A Blueprint for Reforming Automobile Insurance*. Boston: Little, Brown.

Landes, E. M. 1982. "Insurance, Liability, and Accidents: A Theoretical and Empirical Investigation of the Effects of No-Fault Accidents." *Journal of Law and Economics* 25: 49–65.

LeBow, C. C. 1997. "Federalism and Federal Product Liability Reform: A Warning Not Heeded." *Tennessee Law Review* 64: 665–90.

Little, J. W. 1989. "Eliminating the Fallacies of Comparative Negligence and Proportional Liability." *Alabama Law Review* 41: 13–56.

Litras, M. F. X., and C. J. DeFrances. 1999. *Federal Tort Trials and Verdicts, 1996–97*. Washington, D.C.: U.S. Department of Justice, Office of Justice Programs, Bureau of Justice Statistics.

Mahoney, R. 1992. "New Zealand's Accident Compensation Scheme: A Reassessment." *American Journal of Comparative Law* 40: 159–211.

Middleton, R. H. Jr. 2000. "Critique of *New England Journal of Medicine*'s Whiplash Article Promoting No-Fault Auto Insurance." Available at: *www.atlahq.org*. Accessed 4 May 2000.

Nolan, V. E., and E. Ursin. 1995. *Understanding Enterprise Liability*. Philadelphia: Temple University Press.

O'Connell, J. 1975. *Ending Insult to Injury*. Urbana: University of Illinois Press.

———. 1990. "A Model Bill Allowing Choice between Automobile Insurance Payable with or without Regard to Fault." *Ohio State Law Journal* 51: 947–83.

O'Connell, J., S. Carroll, M. Horowitz, A. Abrahamse, and B. Miliauskas. 1996. "Consumer Choice in the North Carolina Auto Insurance Market." *Campbell Law Review* 19: 1–19.

Ostrom, B. J., and N. B. Kander. 1998. *Examining the Work of States Courts: A National Perspective from the Court Statistics Project*. Williamsburg, Va.: National Center for State Courts.

Payne, K. E. 1995. "Linking Tort Reform to Fairness and Moral Values." *Detroit College of Law at Michigan State University Law Review* 1995, no. 4: 1207–46.

Pear, R. 1999. "Protect Patients from Fatal Mistakes, U.S. Urged." *Plain Dealer* (Cleveland), 30 November.

Phillips, J. J. 1985. "In Defense of the Tort System." *Arizona Law Review* 27: 603–16.

———. 1997. "Hoist by One's Own Petard: When a Conservative Commerce Clause Interpretation Meets Conservative Tort Reform." *Tennessee Law Review* 64: 647–64.

———. 1998. *Products Liability in a Nutshell*. 5th ed. St. Paul, Minn.: West Group.

———. 1999. "Commentary on Foibles of the English Language." *Tennessee Law Review* 66: 789–99.

Phillips, J. J., N. Terry, F. Maraist, and F. McClellan. 1997. *Tort Law: Cases, Materials, Problems*. 2d ed. Charlottesville, Va.: Michie.

Platt, F., ed. 1962. *Traffic Safety Research*. Madrid: Fourth World Meeting of International Road Federation.

Rokes, W. 1971. *No-Fault Insurance*. Santa Monica, Calif.: Insurors Press.

Rosenfield, H. 1998. "Auto Insurance: Crisis and Reform." *University of Memphis Law Review* 29: 69–135.

Schermer, I. E. 1995. *Automobile Liability Insurance*. 3d ed. New York: Clark Boardman Callaghan.

Schwartz, G. T. 1994. "Reality in the Economic Analysis of Tort Law: Does Tort Law Really Deter?" *UCLA Law Review* 42: 377–444.

Schwartz, V. E. 1997. *Who Should Make America's Tort Law: Courts or Legislatures?* Washington, D.C.: Washington Legal Foundation.

Shapo, M. S. 1999. "Millennial Torts." *Georgia Law Review* 33: 1021–45.

Sloan, F. A., B. A. Reilley, and C. M. Schenzler. 1994. "Other Approaches for Deterring Careless Driving." *International Review of Law and Economics* 14: 53–71.

———. 1995. "Effects of Tort Liability and Insurance on Heavy Drinking and Drinking and Driving." *Journal of Law and Economics* 38: 49–77.

Tennessee Attorneys Memo. 2000. "Governor Signs Bill for Graduated Licensing System." 25, no. 21 (22 May): 1.

The Underwriters' Wire. 1999. "Record $35.6 Billion After Tax Income; $6.1 Billion Pre-Tax Underwriting Loss." Available at: *www.uwreport.com/wire/news0498/0402rec.htm*. Accessed 10 May 1999.

U.S. Department of Transportation, National Highway Traffic Safety Administration. 1993. "Federal Motor Vehicle Safety Standards; Occupant Crash Protection." *Federal Register* 58, no. 169 (2 September): 46551–68.

U.S. House. 1998. Committee on Commerce. Subcommittee on Finance and Hazardous Materials. *The Auto Choice Reform Act of 1997: Hearings on H.R. 2021*, 105th Cong., 2d sess., 20 May.

U.S. Senate. 1998. Committee on Commerce, Science, and Transportation. *The Auto Choice Reform Act: Hearings on S. 625*, 105th Cong., 2d sess., 9 September.

PART TWO

Stephen Chippendale
The Case for No-Fault Insurance

❏ INTRODUCTION

"James Auffhammer was on the way to a college class when his car brushed the bumper of a Ford Tempo at a stoplight," reports the *Washington Post* (Nguyen 1996). "He paid $27 to repaint the Tempo's bumper and thought that was the end of it. Two years later, the driver of the Ford slapped him with a $400,000 lawsuit claiming the accident caused her severe neck injuries." Eventually, but not until after a full-blown trial, a jury dismissed the lawsuit as meritless.

Auffhammer was able to count his blessings and go home. But taxpayers, consumers, and motorists do not share his good fortune. We are stuck paying every day for these almost endless driver-versus-driver lawsuits.

The automobile insurance available to most Americans combines the worst of both worlds: high costs and low benefits. It promotes excessive litigation (such as the claim against Auffhammer), encourages fraud, over-compensates minor injuries, undercompensates major injuries, and is so expensive that millions drive without insurance. No sane person would intentionally construct this scheme.

No-fault reform, as we shall see, can change this calculus. No-fault insurance provides more comprehensive compensation to injured motorists while saving the rest of us hundreds (if not thousands) of dollars in premiums every year. Few policy initiatives touch the lives of so many Americans.

The import of no fault, I admit, used to escape me. (My youth, alas, was not spent dreaming about auto insurance.) But three experiences conspired to show me the overwhelming importance of no fault—and to lead me to write this essay.

First, at nineteen, I spent a summer as a clerk for the drivers license division of the Missouri Department of Revenue. Seeing the ease with which almost everyone obtains, and renews, their licenses convinced me that Americans are never more likely to get seriously injured than when they are behind the wheel. Accidents are inevitable: Drivers control two-ton vehicles, have little real training, and repeatedly make split-second decisions while distracted by passengers, music, cell phones, and spilt coffee. The surprise is not that there are accidents—it's that there are not even more of them.

Second, at twenty-seven, I finished law school and joined the plaintiffs' firm of Nichols Kaster & Anderson in Minneapolis. It was a real pleasure to practice law with skilled, energetic, and honest attorneys. But I experienced enough personal-injury litigation to learn why *Jurassic Park* audiences cheer when the lawyer gets munched.

Third, at thirty, I traded northern winters for Washington, D.C., and was hired by Mike Horowitz as associate director of the Hudson Institute's Project for Civil Justice Reform. My research there confirmed my earlier belief—auto-accident litigation is a mess.

How big a mess? Americans spend billions of dollars each year on bodily injury premiums (damage to people, not theft or property damage). But only 14.8 percent of these insurance payments are disbursed, as you would expect and as is intended, to accident victims as compensation for medical expenses and lost wages. These payments are almost matched by those for excessive claims (12.6 percent) and almost doubled by outlays to lawyers (28.4 percent).

These numbers are indefensible—and only the tip of the iceberg, notes respected legal columnist Stuart Taylor, Jr. (1998, 1283):

> Imagine a system that takes $350–$1,500 a year from motorists to insure them against liability for bodily injuries; funnels 55 per cent of that to lawyers and insurance companies; pays out most of the rest in "pain and suffering" damages to accident victims; dispenses just 15 per cent to victims for monetary costs such as doctors' bills and lost wages; and grossly undercompensates those with the most-severe injuries.
>
> That's our car insurance system, as shaped by a tort litigation regime that pits driver against driver in a futile quest to assign blame for accidents and provide compensation for intangible injuries that money cannot heal.

As Taylor suggests, the fundamental problem is that the current system provides no incentive for reasonableness. The plaintiff claims the defendant was careless. The defendant claims he was not negligent, but if he was, so was the plaintiff. The defendant's insurer has every reason to resist the claim—the plaintiff is somebody else's customer. Likewise, the plaintiff has no fear of higher premiums to keep her from claiming exaggerated injuries. All of this results in litigation that consumes time and money without compensating victims fairly or efficiently.

Something must be done to allow injured drivers to bypass litigation altogether. The best exit strategy would be widespread adoption of no-fault principles. There is a mountain of evidence supporting the central notion of this essay: that no-fault reform would improve the efficiency and fairness of automobile insurance.

No fault succeeds because it departs from compensation via litigation in two key regards: Lawsuits are curtailed and compensation comes automatically from the accident victim's own insurer. These two changes allow no fault to cut transaction costs and the costs for nonmonetary losses—thereby freeing more money for the injured. As a result, no fault, unlike tort, is a rational and cost-effective means of providing compensation.

Six sections follow. Section 1 begins the body of this essay by sketching the differences between the fault and no-fault approaches to insuring accident victims. Why two approaches? Section 2 answers this question by reporting on the historical and political forces that have kept no fault, despite its greater virtues, the minority insurance system. Sections 3 and 4 operate together. The first describes the erratic compensation and high costs of the fault system; the second explains how greed and lawyers contribute to these problems. Section 5 then explores the archaic notion of "fault" in the context of auto-accident litigation. Finally, section 6 offers an alternative to the litigation trap—an innovative and politically realistic plan for implementing the principles of no-fault insurance.

☐ 1. A TALE OF TWO SYSTEMS

A lawsuit is a fruit tree planted in a lawyer's garden.—*Italian proverb*

Imagine a scene repeated in some variation thousands of times a week: It is Monday morning and you are heading north on Main Street on your way to work. You are drinking coffee, listening to the radio, and thinking about the week ahead. Taking a left, however, you are struck by a car going the other way. The jolt throws you sideways.

You remain in your car until a police officer arrives. The other driver tells the officer that his foot slipped off the brake, but he could not have stopped in time anyway because you pulled out right in front of him. Needless to say, you dispute this account. Then, because your neck and back are hurting, you go to the emergency room. The accident causes you to miss two weeks of work. Ultimately, you suffer economic damages (i.e., lost wages and medical bills) of, say, $15,000.

Will you receive compensation? And, if so, how much?

You may be surprised to learn that these two critical questions are impossible to answer without knowing where you live and what insurance system your state has adopted. In other words, our hypothetical accident begs this question: Is your auto insurance "fault" or "no fault"?

The Fault Approach

Your compensation in the vast majority of states will be determined by tort liability. Tort is known as "fault" because, by lawsuit, you must show the other driver to be in the wrong. A "tort" (literally "twisted") is a wrongful act (other than breach of contract) such as malpractice that causes injury for which the law provides redress. Torts make up the vast bulk of lawsuits between private citizens. And auto accidents constitute the vast bulk of tort claims.

Tort allows you to seek compensation for economic damages (wage loss, medical costs) and noneconomic damages ("pain and suffering") from the person who caused them to the degree that person is found to be responsible. If your lawsuit succeeds, the other driver's liability insurance will pay for these damages up to the policy's limit.

Immediate compensation is available only if the insurance carrier concedes right away that its policyholder was at fault. Such instantaneous harmony is unusual. More than 90 percent of drivers in two-car accidents say the other driver was at fault—and, remarkably, more than one-third of drivers try to blame someone else in *one-car* accidents (Hensler et al. 1991, 159). In short, after an accident, drivers pass the buck whenever possible.

Most likely, then, the answer to what you do after the accident is a time-honored American tradition: You hire a lawyer. To find one, you scour the Yellow Pages for someone who represents accident victims (colloquially known as a "trial lawyer"). You meet with several, and each offers the same terms: No fee unless there is a recovery, in which case the attorney will take one-third of the gross, leaving the litigation expenses (photocopying, transcripts, and so on) to you. The lawyer you eventually retain is a modern-day Robin Hood—but a Robin who will keep a chunk of the recovery.

After being hired, your lawyer files suit in state court alleging that the other driver's negligence caused you grave injuries (some of which you may first learn about when reviewing the complaint). The other driver is served with the papers and passes them on to the lawyer provided by his insurance company. (Each accident thus employs at least two lawyers—and more if additional cars are involved or countersuits are filed.)

Discovery ensues. Medical records are produced. You and the other driver are deposed. Your spouse is deposed about your mental state. Your doctors are deposed. You undergo an "adverse" medical examination.

A year passes and your attorney becomes concerned about the pending trial. She will have the burden of showing that the other driver was at fault, and who knows what the jury will think? If it finds against you, there is no recovery. And even if it finds for you, she may not receive a fee of much more than $5,000 (one-third of the economic injuries of $15,000). For a lawyer with many cases, a trial becomes a lot of work for just $5,000.

The defense lawyer is also concerned. He would hate to be embarrassed in court. Also, who knows what the jury will do? You seem like a sympathetic person to whom the jury may award a large (and unpredictable) pain-and-suffering award.

The mutual fear of trial thus prompts a conference where the parties reach a $20,000 settlement. You agree to this amount to avoid the possibility of the jury awarding less; the insurance company agrees to avoid the jury awarding more.

You do not pocket the $20,000. Instead, your lawyer first takes her one-third share (almost $7,000) and then you pay the litigation costs, about $2,000. (And, depending on the state, your insurance company may have the right to recover any money it has already paid you for the accident.) Thus, one year after the accident, you receive about $11,000 for $15,000 in actual loss.

Our hypothetical accident illustrates several important characteristics of the fault system. If you are injured in an accident, your compensation hinges on your ability to demonstrate the other driver's negligence. If you win, the other driver (actually his or her insurance company) pays you for your medical costs, lost wages, and pain and suffering. If you lose, you get nothing. Either way, delay is likely, your lawyer will "tax" any recovery, the jury verdict will depend on the evidence and the relative skills of the lawyers, and the burden is on you, the victim, to prove the case.

The fault system is something only a lawyer or Rube Goldberg could love. Now let us consider the alternative: no-fault insurance.

The No-Fault Approach

No fault recognizes that faultfinding eats up time and money that could—and should—be spent compensating accident victims. Under no fault, therefore, you do not need to prove someone else's responsibility before you get paid, and payment is limited to actual loss. By shifting to first-party policies limited to economic loss, no fault eliminates the two main lawsuit tussles: who is at fault and what pain is worth.

While slashing the need for lawyers, no fault also fills in tort's compensation gaps. Had a one-car accident? Found at "fault" for the accident? If so, under the tort system, you are out of luck. Not so under no fault.

Unlike our imaginary Monday morning collision, the difference between a third-party, liability-based compensation mechanism and one based on first-party, automatic insurance compensation is not hypothetical. It can make a real difference in the lives of accident victims. Just how much can be seen in two cases—one in Illinois, the other in Michigan—cited by *Consumer Reports* ("Whatever Happened to No-Fault?" 1984).

In Illinois, a young man suffered permanent brain damage when his car smashed into a highway divider after he fell asleep at the wheel. Because the state operates under the tort system, and there was no one to sue and no auto-insurance coverage, health insurance picked up part of the medical bills, but his family was responsible for rehabilitation costs. Three years after the accident, they were paying $1,500 a month with no assistance in sight.

In Michigan, a car struck a young girl from behind while she was riding her bicycle. She too suffered permanent brain damage. Unlike Illinois, however, Michigan has the nation's most comprehensive no-fault law. The family's insurance carrier picked up the entire tab for medical expenses and rehabilitation (almost $200,000) because the policy extended to accidents on a bicycle. The family paid nothing for medical care and rehabilitation treatment.

To be sure, if the girl lived in a tort state, her family could have sued the driver. But tort awards are essentially limited to the amount of the other driver's liability coverage. In some states, the mandated minimum is only $15,000. Of course, the driver may have taken out insurance exceeding the minimum, but it is unlikely that the driver would have been taken out a $200,000 policy. (And, in fact, the driver did not have paid-up insurance.)

No fault frees you from having your insurance coverage decided by others—and you can afford more comprehensive coverage because you are not paying for lawyers. The reimbursement is automatic, but not lavish: It does not pay for "pain and suffering," it caps the amount of recoverable lost wages (you can sue for excess amounts), and it pays bills when they are due instead of providing claimants a lump sum that can sometimes make lotto winners blush.

Thus, if our hypothetical accident were in a no-fault state, you would go to your own insurance company instead of a lawyer. There is no lawsuit. Neither you nor the other driver is sued or has to sue the other to receive compensation. The issue of fault, that is, who caused the accident, is not relevant (hence "no fault"). Reckless drivers still go to jail and see their insurance premiums soar, but your compensation does not depend on successfully pressing a claim against an adequately insured driver.

First-party insurance is identical to life, health, and home. No lawyers. No lawsuits. No gambling that the other driver has sufficient insurance. All of these are features of no-fault insurance. No fault is a system for everyone except lawyers.

These virtues raise the question of why the debate over auto insurance was not resolved long ago in favor of no fault. Why is it likely that your state subjects you to the whims (and costs) of the tort system? The next section's short history lesson answers this question.

☐ 2. A BRIEF HISTORY OF NO FAULT

The one charm of the past is that it is the past.—Oscar Wilde

Accidents and automobiles have always been inseparable. In 1896, when there were only four cars in the entire country, two were in St. Louis. And they collided (O'Connell 1971).

Cars were the first great innovation of the twentieth century. Nothing was the same after Henry Ford built his company in 1901—a transformation documented by Orson Wells in *The Magnificent Ambersons*. The horseless carriage changed how Americans work and play—as well as suffer and die.

Policymakers have long recognized that cars combine catastrophe and convenience. But to diagnose is not to cure. Multiple approaches to aiding accident victims have been explored for almost a century. A brief review of these efforts provides needed perspective to the current debate over the merits of no-fault insurance.

Financial Responsibility Laws and Mandatory Insurance

Many Americans did not greet the Model T with open arms (Richards 1949). It did not help that nighttime collisions between cars and carriages were so prevalent that one state prohibited the use of motor vehicles between dusk and dawn. An extract from a 1904 law journal gives the flavor:

> Many [cars] are operated by persons who may be fitly described as wealthy hoodlums. These fellows drive their powerful machines along country roads with insolent disregard of the rights of other travelers. . . . A judge of the supreme court, driving a spirited team [of horses] was recently compelled to

check the furious onrush of one of the "devil wagons" by jumping to the ground, getting to the head of his team, and, after, signaling in vain, to threaten the automobilist with rocks, before he would slacken speed ("Reckless Automobilists" 1904, 432).

When confronted by the new "devil wagons" and their inevitable accidents, courts reacted by turning to negligence. As discussed in section 1, this principle allocates legal "fault" among the parties to an accident.

This allocation could perhaps be justified when cars were novelties because those able to afford them were also able to assume the risk of injury to others.[1] (Note, for example, that the law journal quoted above refers to motorists as "wealthy hoodlums.") But cars did not remain the province of the wealthy for long; they soon beat out carriages for a place in America's heart and on its roads. Eventually car ownership, or at least driving, became the rule rather than the exception. And as driving became widespread, more and more drivers lacked the financial wherewithal to compensate accident victims. In Boston, to cite only one city, car fatalities increased by 800 percent in the decade after 1909, and injuries rose about 500 percent (Rollins 1919, 392).

Prompted by horror tales about destitute victims, states, beginning in the 1920s, attempted to modify a woefully deficient tort-compensation system. But reveille rather than taps was played for the tort system. Instead of abandoning negligence, legislatures adopted so-called financial-responsibility laws to supplement the common law.

These new regulations—future-proof laws and security-deposit laws—prodded car owners into obtaining liability insurance (Widiss et al. 1977, 1–7). Future-proof laws required a driver, after an accident, to prove an ability to satisfy a judgment arising from a *future* accident. Security-deposit laws, on the other hand, required a driver to post security for a judgment resulting from his or her *first* accident.

Connecticut adopted the first future-proof law in 1925 (Meeks 1998). Any driver in an accident causing $100 of damage had to prove an ability to satisfy a future claim for $10,000. Other states adopted similar schemes. But these laws affected only a small number of motorists—perhaps two dozen of every 10,000 registered vehicles.

Security-deposit laws become more common. In these states every owner deposited security as compensation for any injuries caused in a first accident. But the requirement applied only if the owner lacked liability insurance that met the state's minimum requirements.

As a practical matter, then, by the 1950s, mandatory insurance had displaced the financial-responsibility laws (Widiss et al. 1977, 16). But, then as now, liability coverage is not a self-executing distribution mechanism for compensating victims. Nor does it prevent an owner from allowing the insurance to lapse after registration. An awareness of these limitations—as well as of the continuing failure of the tort system, even augmented by insurance, to compensate adequately the seriously injured—led to a rekindling of no-fault insurance.

The Rise of No Fault

Although no fault made headlines in the late 1960s and early 1970s, the concept was not new. Indeed, while the Model T was still in production, observers realized that fault compensation was costly and ineffective. A year after World War I, my old journal, the *Minnesota Law Review*, published what is generally recognized as the first call for applying "no-fault" principles in auto accidents. The prescient lawyer-author wrote:

> [T]he general aim should be to eliminate entirely the question of negligence in motor vehicle accidents; to make certain and payable at all events a reasonable compensation . . . spreading the cost of such compensation over all users of motor vehicles on the public highways; and to provide a summary method of determining the amount of such losses (Carmen 1919, 2).

Workers' Compensation Model

The Minnesota author and other would-be reformers found inspiration in workers' compensation insurance. This system provided a useful model for several reasons, one of which was that it had taken hold just a few years earlier.

Before workers' compensation, injured employees depended on their employers' goodwill or on winning a lawsuit (Lewiston 1967, 198–99). Neither was likely. Bosses tended to be tightfisted and courts interposed formidable obstacles to litigation. A lawsuit was possible only if the employer was directly negligent, the employee's negligence did not contribute to the accident, the employee had not (expressly or impliedly) assumed the risk of injury, *and* the accident was not the result of a fellow worker's negligence. A stringent standard, to say the least.

Workers' compensation did away with the onerous burden imposed on employees by adopting the principle of liability without fault (Hood and Hardy 1983, 23–38). It assumed that accidents are inevitable and their costs should be part of the total cost of doing business. Under the schemes put in place at the turn of the century, and in effect today, medical, cash, and sometimes rehabilitation benefits are paid to a worker hurt on the job regardless of whether the employee or the employer (or both) was at fault.

This universal insurance is built around two trade-offs (Mooney 1989, 78). Employees give up pain-and-suffering litigation in exchange for automatic payment of their medical bills and lost wages. Employers, in turn, surrender their ability to contest damages or responsibility in exchange for litigation immunity for job-related accidents.

To be sure, workers' compensation is not perfect (it is a trade-off, after all), but almost everyone wins under its no-fault scheme. By cutting litigation, costs are cut, time is saved, and injured people receive immediate compensation. It certainly beats requiring workers to file lawsuits over the most mundane accidents—a system that would exist were automobile insurance the model.

Early Calls for Reform

A 1932 report published by Columbia University indicted the tort system as expensive, wasteful, and slow. The authors unequivocally recommended adoption of a replacement system based on workers' compensation. Contributing to a symposium, the study's director continued the argument:

> For automobile accidents, a system of compensation without regard to fault, administered like workmen's compensation, would be better than the present system of liability for negligence only; because it is no longer realistic to apply the negligence test to automobile compensation; because such a system would more fairly distribute losses, particularly in serious cases; because payments would be prompter; and because the courts in the large cities would be relieved of a mass of litigation which is no longer suited for jury trial (Lewis 1936, 597).

The Columbia study received serious consideration in at least four states: Connecticut, New York, Virginia, and Wisconsin (Greer 1992). But intensive lobbying kept the proposal from being adopted (although it did influence a no-fault scheme implemented in part of Canada). Many thought this failure tragic:

> One dead every 15 minutes. One injured every 22 seconds. Every year the injured and dead equal the population of St. Louis. Four years delay in New York. Five years delay in Chicago. Delay everywhere. Hospitals crowded with

automobile victims. No improvement in the whole miserable system in thirty years. In that period—the radio, television, the atom—all new. The new has displaced the old—but we lawyers still cling with petrified thoughts to the dead hand of the archaic liability system—devised for the dead past (Marx 1954, 159–60).

In the early 1960s a group of academics within the aegis of the University of Pennsylvania updated the Columbia study (Morris and Paul 1962). Sampling accidents that occurred outside Philadelphia in Lancaster County, the researchers found the tort system still inefficient. Of the surveyed accident victims, for instance, almost a quarter (23.9 percent) had received absolutely no compensation. As a result, the researchers concluded that "tort law in action—the business of securing awards—is fraught with delay and uncertainty [and] its generosities are largely reserved for the trivially injured" (p. 924).

Other studies echoed this conclusion, but tort remained in place. The roads became congested, insurance costs soared, and by December 1951 the United States had experienced its one-millionth traffic fatality (James and Law 1952, 71). But the no-fault concept remained fallow until cultivated by two law professors: Robert E. Keeton and Jeffrey O'Connell.

Keeton–O'Connell

In their seminal study, published in 1965 under the title *Basic Protection for the Traffic Victim*, Keeton and O'Connell concluded that the fault system was a crapshoot for the injured: Some received too little compensation and others too much. To remedy the flawed tort system, the professors advanced a no-fault blueprint worth highlighting in some detail because it forms the basis for much of the current debate.

Keeton and O'Connell proposed the "development of a new form of compulsory automobile insurance (called basic protection insurance), which in its nature is an extension of the principle of medical payments coverage" (p. 5). The insurance would compensate "all persons injured in automobile accidents without regard to fault for all types of out-of-pocket personal injury losses up to certain limits" (p. 5). They proposed "granting to basic protection insureds an exemption from tort liability . . . in those cases which damages would not exceed the $10,000 limit of basic protection coverage [about $35,000 today]" (p. 5). A lawsuit could be brought, however, for any out-of-pocket loses not compensated by the basic protection.

The plan's central theme was that fault liability should be removed and a system of first-party insurance substituted in its place. Under the proposal, auto-accident victims (much like injured workers) would forsake lawsuits except in serious cases. In return, they would receive swift compensation for medical expenses, lost wages, and other economic damages—but nothing for noneconomic damages. The new system would pay for itself by reducing systemwide costs. Keeton and O'Connell explained:

> The exemption [from tort liability] drastically reduces the number of cases in which the expense of litigation and preparation for the prospect of litigation will be incurred, since the percentage of injuries so severe as to escape applicability of the tort exemption is small. The effect on both court congestion and the administrative overhead of an automobile claims system will be distinctly beneficial (p. 275).

In other words, the costs of prosecuting and defending claims and paying wildcard "pain-and-suffering" damages would disappear except in more serious cases. More money would then be free for more victims.

Implementing Keeton–O'Connell

History repeated itself: The Keeton–O'Connell plan did not ignite reform. The authors were professors after all, not politicians, and they were taking on a savvy opponent girded for combat. An indication of the opposition can be seen in the *New York Times*: "In state after state, the [no-fault] plan has been defeated or bottled up in committees, often through the efforts of powerful lobbies of lawyers' groups and insurance companies, both of which are heavily represented among members of state legislatures" (King 1970, 70).

Fortunately, however, one of Keeton's students was Michael Dukakis, who went on to the Massachusetts legislature, three terms as governor, and the Democratic presidential nomination. Richard Ben Cramer explains in his masterly *What It Takes* (1992, 512) how Dukakis used the Keeton–O'Connell plan to launch his political career:

> Dukakis . . . was the first to promote the new concept of no fault insurance. Small cases would never get to court. A driver would collect from his own insurance—without regard to fault. This would streamline the courts, put money into the pockets of the aggrieved, and cut the cost of premiums in Massachusetts (at that time, the highest in the nation). This was not ideological, it was simply rational—in other words, vintage Dukakis.
>
> Of course, no one thought he could do it. The lawyers, the insurance companies—they *loved* the old system. But they did not reckon with Dukakis, who went at this like a steam piston.

Finally, on 1 January 1971, after a political compromise was brokered in Boston, the nation's first no-fault automobile insurance bill went into effect (Mooney 1989, 79). Its essence was that lawsuits could not be filed unless claimants had already exhausted their $2,000 of no-fault benefits or spent more than $500 on medical expenses.

Après Massachusetts, le déluge. No fault was quickly adopted by several states. It is no exaggeration to say no fault was *the* insurance issue of the early 1970s. Two trial lawyers, for example, published a book lamenting "the drive to institute no fault . . . across the country" (Gillespie and Klipper 1972, 155).

The Fall of No Fault(?)

The whirl of legislative action obscured the fact that the prototype Massachusetts law was a tattered version of the Keeton–O'Connell plan. The original bill provided for $10,000 worth of benefits; the state legislature cut that figure to $2,000. The bill also wiped out all lawsuits unless the pain and suffering of the victim exceeded $5,000; the legislature cut that figure to $500. Each revision opened the door to litigation.

This inability of legislators to keep fault out of their ostensibly "no-fault" plans proved to be the Achilles' heel of the early 1970s movement. All of the reform states retained pain-and-suffering lawsuits for accidents exceeding certain "threshold" levels. These thresholds are discussed below. Suffice it to say that they undermined a fundamental principle of Keeton–O'Connell: that drivers should insure themselves.

The blending of fault and no-fault principles meant that insurance costs went up instead of down. The "no-fault" states had higher costs because, in effect, drivers were paying for two systems. Accident victims could automatically collect from their own insurance carrier (unlike under tort) but could also easily sue (unlike under true no fault). Nonetheless, as the U.S. Department of Transportation documented in 1985, even these small, tentative steps toward no fault were in the right direction. Here are some of the Department's conclusions after a dozen years of experimentation:

- "Significantly more motor vehicle accident victims receive auto insurance compensation in no fault States than in other States."
- "In general, accident victims in no fault States have access to a greater amount of money from auto insurance than victims in traditional States."

■ "Compensation payments under no fault insurance are made far more swiftly than under traditional auto insurance."

■ "No fault insurance systems pay a greater percentage of premium income to injured claimants than do traditional liability systems."

Why the Drive for No Fault Stalled

Given no fault's success, and its even greater promise, why are states reluctant to do away with the fault system?

One answer is that no fault was a victim of its compromised early success. When the flawed reforms did not reduce premiums, the politically birthed laws, no fault in name only, were exploited to discredit the entire no-fault concept:

> [T]rial lawyer lobbying has helped convince . . . states to enact what is called weak no fault—which is actually worse than [no no-fault] at all. In weak no fault states the threshold of accident seriousness is set so low—sometimes at a mere hundred dollars of medical bills—that any lawyer can get his client into court just by sending him to a cooperative doctor for a battery of tests. . . . Insurance rates rise to cover the costs of running two compensation systems at once. Trial lawyers and their allies among supposed consumer advocates then gleefully proclaim that no fault has failed (Olson 1991, 309).

As its very fond uncle, O'Connell is a close observer of no fault's political fortunes. He attributes its complete defeat in some states, and enactment in watered-down form in others, to the influential role lawyers play in the public arena (e.g., 1979; O'Connell and Kelly 1987). O'Connell is far from alone in crediting lawyers with snuffing the early promise of no fault (Tobias 1993; Mooney 1989). Lawyers, after all, are traditionally the largest professional group within legislatures (O'Connell and Kelly 1987, 118). These lawyers-legislators are able to argue against no fault in committee and then vote against it on the floor.

That lawyers desire to do away with no fault is understandable because no fault desires to do away with lawyers. Lawyers who promote no fault do so against their profession's self-interest. Asking lawyers to support no fault is like asking mechanics to endorse an engine that never needs servicing.

"The group that stands to lose the most from no fault legislation is the trial bar (which earns more than $1 billion a year in automobile accident fees alone)" (Bok 1993, 143). With this vested economic interest, the Association of Trial Lawyers of America (ATLA), which is an interest group composed largely of plaintiffs' personal-injury lawyers, had led the crusade against no fault. Besides funding the fight, ATLA also distributes a hand-book—*Identifying and Neutralizing No-Fault Legislation* (Wend et al. n.d.)—which has chapters such as "How to Counterattack" and "What to Do When They Say: 'No Fault Saves Legal Fees.'"

Flawed experiments and interest-group opposition, in short, contrib-uted to the no-fault movement cresting in the mid-1970s.[2] No state has adopted no fault since 1976; indeed, five states abrogated their no-fault laws between 1980 and 1991 (Greer 1992). The federal *No Fault Motor Vehicle Insurance Act* passed the Senate in 1974 only to fail in the House of Representatives. More recently, in California's 1996 primary elections, trial lawyers led a successful campaign against Proposition 200, which would have established a true no-fault system (Tobias 1997, 70–115). Pure no fault thus remains a dream—albeit one that is eighty years old.

The State of No Fault

Today, in thirty-seven states, tort liability is the only insurance option available to motorists. The remaining thirteen states use a variety of no-fault systems. In other words, there are two "tort" states for every "no-fault" one.

To be sure, some observers suggest the balance is really twenty-six tort and twenty-four no fault (the thirteen states above plus eleven "add-on" ones: Arkansas, Delaware, Maryland, New Hampshire, Oregon, South Caro-lina, South Dakota, Texas, Virginia, Washington, and Wisconsin). But this counting method ignores that add-on plans are not no fault. Add-on schemes simply offer modest no-fault benefits without limiting lawsuits; there is no trade-off between reduced litigation and higher benefits (Meeks 1998, 15). Ironically, the add-on benefits help finance lawsuits because the up-front payments allow plaintiffs to wait during litigation.

Only a baker's dozen of states, then, can be considered no fault: Colorado, Florida, Hawaii, Kansas, Kentucky, Massachusetts, Michigan, Min-nesota, New Jersey, New York, North Dakota, Pennsylvania, and Utah. Each couples the payment of first-party benefits with some restrictions on lawsuits for noneconomic damages. These benefits and "thresholds" are illustrated in Table 1.

Table 1 highlights that no-fault states employ two different thresholds for screening litigation: monetary and descriptive. Monetary thresholds are most common. In eight states, lawsuits are allowed only when a minimum amount of medical expenses is exceeded. Monetary thresholds range from $1,000 (in Kentucky) to $5,000 (in Hawaii). (Minnesota's threshold is varied:

TABLE 1. No-Fault States

State	Threshold
Colorado	$2,500 in medical bills
Florida	Descriptive
Hawaii	$5,000 in medical bills
Kansas	$2,000 in medical bills
Kentucky*	$1,000 in medical bills
Massachusetts	$2,000 in medical bills
Michigan	Descriptive
Minnesota	$4,000 in medical bills
New Jersey*	Descriptive
New York	Descriptive
North Dakota	$2,500 in medical bills
Pennsylvania*	Descriptive
Utah	$3,000 in medical bills

*Choice states where residents may select a system with no lawsuit restrictions.

death, permanent injury, or disfigurement; more than $4,000 in medical bills; or at least sixty days of disability.) Generally speaking, the higher the threshold, the lower the premium.

Problems abound. Most fundamentally, the thresholds are ineffective—litigation remains routine. The fixed-dollar amounts also create an incentive for claim padding: Claimants scale them with the determination of mountaineers. But sometimes inflation does the job for them. In Massachusetts, where prior to 1988 the threshold was $500, the percentage of potential litigants eligible to sue in tort increased from 26.3 percent in 1977 to 53.5 percent in 1987 (Greer 1992, 275).

The solution, as Pennsylvania illustrates, is unfortunately not as simple as just increasing the threshold amounts (Mooney 1989). The state's original "no-fault" plan allowed lawsuits when medical expenses exceeded $750—a low threshold that allowed many accident victims to file both no-fault and tort claims. Premiums rose about 20 percent annually to cover costs. When the legislature attempted to raise the threshold, and thereby lower costs, attorneys objected. Caught between this powerful lobby and upset voters, legislators did not steal a page from Churchill; they threw in the towel. The state removed all restrictions on lawsuits (although a "freedom-of-choice" law discussed in section 6 was later adopted).

Descriptive (or verbal) thresholds better approximate the spirit of true no fault. These statutes use words instead of numbers to define when an injury is sufficiently serious to justify a pain-and-suffering lawsuit. A verbal threshold typically requires would-be litigants to prove a "serious impairment of body function" or a "permanent serious disfigurement." (Death is the third category.) Claimants with lesser injuries are compensated only for economic loss through first-party insurance and then by lawsuit for any excess amounts.

Michigan and New York are generally regarded as having the most effective verbal thresholds (Segal 1993, 28). Adoption of Michigan's threshold, for instance, resulted in the percentage of premium dollars paid to lawyers dropping from 32 percent to 4 percent, and the percentage paid to claimants rising from 48 percent to 73 percent. Similarly, New York's threshold resulted in case filings plunging 80 percent and premium prices dropping 6 percent.

No fault's effectiveness in these two states continues to this day. Importantly, premiums have risen slower than inflation, probably because Michigan and New York have contained costs by screening out illegitimate claims. The rate of illegitimacy may be seen by comparing the number of physical injuries claimed to the total number of collisions occurring under the different insurance regimes. In states with low monetary thresholds, claimants are twice as likely to claim that they have been physically injured than in descriptive no-fault states (e.g., New York and Michigan); in add-on states, claimants are three times more likely to claim a bodily injury; and in tort states claimants are four times more likely to claim a bodily injury. Stated a little differently, in no-fault states only one out of ten people in a car accident assert that they have been injured, whereas in tort states four out of ten people assert such injuries (Foppert 1992). If claimants believe they can easily obtain excessive payment for unverified claims, they are much more likely to pursue these claims—whether or not they are legitimate.

Verbal thresholds, however, are not perfect. Their effectiveness turns on whether the courts begin to relax the threshold requirement (known as "slippage"). Traditionally, New York and Michigan courts have kept litigation under control by narrowly defining "serious injury." In *Licari v. Elliot* (441 N.E.2d 1088 (N.Y. 1982)), for instance, the appellate court held that a cab driver could not file suit over a sprain that kept him from his household chores. In Florida, however, the threshold is less effective because courts have allowed suits over "permanent" injuries even if they are not "serious." And (surprise!) "it appears that more and more people are getting more and more permanent injuries in automobile accidents in Florida" (Foppert 1992, 22).

Every year that verbal thresholds are in place lawyers become more adept at climbing over them. This training can be seen in New York's rising bodily injury/property damage ratio, which increased almost 50 percent between 1989 and 1993 (Insurance Research Council 1996a, table A-34). Nonetheless, in 1992, an English lawyer reviewing the American insurance system concluded:

> To an outside observer, . . . it does seem that Keeton and O'Connell's underlying theory is still valid; at some point reducing the right to sue in tort seems a fair and sensible trade-off for providing more frequent payments for net economic losses on a no fault basis. And indeed the general verdict in the United States does appear to be that no fault has been a success in Michigan and New York—and possibly also in Florida and one or two other jurisdictions (Greer 1992, 275).

In sum, the principal failing of no-fault plans is their failure to reduce premiums.[3] But against this debit must be placed several credits: First, no-fault states deliver a higher proportion of premium dollars to claimants than do tort states. For each premium dollar, no-fault states pay 50.2 cents in victim benefits as opposed to the 43.2 cents paid in tort states (Hager 1998; U.S. Department of Transportation 1985). Second, no-fault states deliver insurance compensation to more automobile accident victims than do tort states. Some estimates conclude that almost twice as many accident victims are compensated under no fault as under tort (Hager 1998; U.S. Department of Transportation 1985, 83). And third, no-fault states deliver compensation more quickly than do tort states. Within one year of filing their claim, the average no-fault claimant receives 95 percent of her recovery while the average tort claimant just about 50 percent (Hager 1998; Joost 1992).

Cost savings and victim compensation are greatest when no fault is closest to pure. But no state has adopted a pure no-fault approach to compensating accident victims (Jasper 1996). Every state maintains litigation. It does not give away too much of what follows in the next three sections to say that I think this is a mistake.

❑ 3. THE FAULTS OF FAULT

> A small town that can't support one lawyer can always support two.
> —*Charles Lamb*

Mark Twain once remarked that liars could be divided into three categories: liars, damned liars, and statisticians. But some statistics speak truthfully. Among them are two facts that demonstrate the fault system's disrepair:

- Auto-accident victims with damages over $100,000 get back, on average, just nine cents on the dollar (Carroll, Kakalik, Pace, and Adams 1991, 22).
- About one-third of claimed medical costs are excessive and unnecessary, costing consumers $13 billion to $18 billion per year, or about $130 per auto-insurance policy (Carroll, Abrahamse, and Vaiana 1995, 23).

These numbers are compelling—and incomplete. Many additional statistics confirm that the fault system "ill serves the accident victim, the insuring public, and society. It is inefficient, overly costly, incomplete, and slow. It allocates benefits poorly, discourages rehabilitation, and overburdens the courts and the legal system" (U.S. Department of Transportation 1971, 100).

Under the tort system, if you sue successfully, you will receive money for both your economic loss and your pain and suffering. But determining fault and putting a price on pain is often problematic. This leads to expensive litigation, with lawyers as intermediaries, and compensation that can be unfair, inefficient, and dilatory.

We now examine these problems. This section describes how tort fails to compensate victims while imposing high costs on everyone else. The next section reviews the role of greed and lawyers in a system riddled with delay and fraud. Section 5 then examines the underlying rational for the "current system"—fault—and explains why it is deeply flawed.

Distorted Compensation

Our review of auto-insurance systems is based on the touchstone that compensating accident victims is the raison d'être for insurance. Indeed, the very word "insurance" means to be indemnified against loss or damage.[4] Thus, the principal measure of success (or failure) is the extent to which injured individuals receive swift and sufficient compensation.

By this standard, tort is a disaster. Like latter-day Goldilocks', accident victims receive too much compensation, too little, or nothing at all. Very rarely is the succor just right.

This distorted compensation is a by-product of how compensation is provided to injured motorists. Victims do not file claims with their insurance companies; they sue. This litigation prerequisite is an aberration. Most insurance coverage—home, health, and so on—is first party: People insure themselves. Auto insurance, in contrast, is third party: Compensation is paid to someone other than the policyholder. Under this system, which bases recovery on establishing legal fault, lawyers must be hired and lawsuits filed.

Tort's reliance on litigation benefits accident victims with minor injuries: They make out like proverbial bandits. Accidents are moneymaking events for them because it is cheaper for insurance companies to settle small claims than to fight them in court. As a result, people with economic losses under $5,000 typically recover two or three times their actual losses (Carroll, Kakalik, Pace, and Adams 1991).

Nothing in life is free, and this is true for automobile insurance. A cumulative consequence of the system's generosity to the barely injured is that money is sapped away from the people who really need help—the seriously injured. Unfortunately, as cited at the beginning of this section, accident victims with more than $100,000 in damages recover, on average, just 9 percent of their loss. Andrew Tobias (1997) notes that if this were true for a homeowner's policy, a policyholder would receive two and one-half lamps each time one was broken, but only nine cents on the dollar if her house burnt to the ground.

This inadequate compensation is explained, in part, by how the current system calls for drivers to insure each other. Lacking an incentive to protect their own well-being, motorists routinely skimp on their liability coverage. Moreover, depending on the state, 15 percent to 30 percent of all drivers are without liability insurance (Carroll and Abrahamse 1998, 13).

Many other motorists carry only the state-mandated insurance because even the minimum is expensive (especially if they have accident histories) and because of low incomes (and thus few assets to protect). Although strictly speaking these drivers are not uninsured, they are not fully insured. The mandated coverage in some states is only $15,000, leaving the injured driver just $10,000 after attorney fees are paid. Overall, the average U.S. driver—a composite of Donald Trump and uninsureds—is on the road with about $60,000 of liability insurance. No wonder the seriously injured go without full compensation.

Table 2 highlights litigation's distorted compensation. Between the extremes are the victims with an economic loss of $25,000 to $100,000. These individuals receive back just over one-half of their losses (Carroll, Kakalik, Pace, and Adams 1991, 22). Thus, if you have, say, $25,000 in economic losses, you can expect to receive only $13,000 in compensation.

TABLE 2. Compensation as a Percent of Economic Loss under the Tort System

Size of Loss	Percent
$500 to $1,000	250
$25,000 to $100,000	56
Over $100,000	9

Source: Joint Economic Committee 1997, 3.

Table 2 reflects the results of section 1's hypothetical accident. In that case, after filing suit and litigating for one year, you, the accident victim, collect $11,000 in compensation for $15,000 in actual loss, or just 73 percent.

This distortion is an intractable part of an insurance system built around litigation. Do not expect the numbers to improve. Decades ago, studies of the reparations paid to automobile-accident victims also found that tort undercompensates large losses and overcompensates small ones. For example, one study in the late 1960s concluded that victims with small economic losses recovered, on average, nearly twice their loss, but those with high economic losses ($25,000 and over) recovered only one-fifth (Galanter 1996, 1117). The difference between that 1960s trend and the one in Table 2 is that inflation has increased the amount of money it takes for an injury to be considered severe.

But the undercompensated are more fortunate than people unable to find a scapegoat—they receive nothing. About *30 percent* of all accident victims recover nothing under the fault system (Carroll and Abrahamse 1998, 11). This yawning gap in coverage—almost one of every three victims—is easily explained. It takes two to sue. If your car is the only one involved in the accident, then you are out of luck. There is no coverage, for instance, if your car skids on the ice and hits a tree. You cannot sue yourself. In 1993, a typical year, one-car accidents constituted 59.9 percent of all fatal accidents and 32.1 percent of all injury-causing accidents (Joost 1992, 44). It is a badge of shame for the fault system that it leaves these victims out in the cold.

Costs and Consequences

"The rich," noted F. Scott Fitzgerald, "are different from you and me." "Yes," riposted Ernest Hemingway, "they have more money." To this famous, if apocryphal, exchange may be appended: "Yes, they can afford liability insurance."

Almost all car owners have to reach deep into their pockets to cover the high cost of insurance. Since 1982 premiums have grown at about twice the rate of inflation. From 1987 to 1992, the cost of auto insurance for private vehicles increased 37.5 percent, an average annual increase of 6.3 percent (Joost 1992, 45). In some urban centers—Miami and Philadelphia, for example—a driver may pay $2,000 a year on a three-year-old car worth at best $8,000 (Berte 1991, 1).

Premiums soar despite ever-safer cars because of the tort tax. Simply put, drivers pay for the rampant litigation as carriers apportion their tort costs to each premium just as stores raise prices to cover shoplifting. Two economists (Cummins and Tennyson 1992, 107) explain this inflation:

> The legal environment plays a critical role in driving up auto insurance costs. It is too easy and too profitable to file bodily injury claims on auto insurance. In tort states and low-threshold no fault states, motorists experiencing minor accidents effectively receive a lottery ticket. The ticket gives them a high probability of winning some amount of money (like $5,000) and a low probability of no gain. The lottery winnings are the motorist's share of a general damage (pain and suffering) award. The price of the ticket is either zero or a small positive amount.

Congress's Joint Economic Committee (JEC; 1996, 2) agrees: "[A]s tort costs continue to skyrocket, all drivers pay the price through higher automobile insurance premiums." Supportive evidence is abundant. For example, in the suburbs of Camden, New Jersey, a married couple with one car and a seventeen-year-old daughter must pay more than $2,000 a year for relatively good coverage. But this is cheap compared to the $4,700 paid annually by a two-car family in Pasadena, California, where each parent has one speeding ticket and the seventeen-year-old son is an occasional driver. Overall, data from the Bureau of Labor Statistics indicate, remarkably, that middle-income families spend twice as much on vehicle insurance as on education (Joint Economic Committee 1998, 32–33).

The high costs are indisputable. What about the consequences? Some may seek to dismiss this question by observing that driving is a privilege rather than a right. And, of course, the Bill of Rights does not guarantee affordable car insurance. But this posture is harsh and unrealistic. Harsh because it ignores that we live in the Age of the Auto; unrealistic because it ignores our uncertain commitment to mass transit. "Getting into our cars is like getting into our clothes—a daily necessity. . . . There are no possessions, other than our homes, upon which we Americans rely more than on our cars, vans, and trucks" (Johnston 1997, 4).

A societal imperative exists to make auto insurance affordable to all Americans. The necessity of such an offering is underscored by the problem of uninsured motorists and the harmful relationship between the fault system and cities, low-income drivers, government, and business.

The Problem of Uninsured Drivers

Low-income drivers face a special dilemma. They can obey the law and purchase liability coverage, thereby depleting their limited resources to buy insurance protecting a *stranger*. Or they can save their money by doing something that is a criminal offense in almost every state: Drive uninsured. This unpalatable choice is sketched by an editorial published in the *Philadelphia Tribune* (and cited by Congress):

> There is one issue that impacts more Philadelphians than all the crimes committed in any given month and that is the (criminal) auto insurance rates Philadelphians are *forced* to pay simply because they live within the city.
>
> Because state law mandates that motor vehicle owners must have insurance to drive these vehicles and because many Philadelphians are required to pay auto insurance rates far in excess of the value of the vehicles they drive, many Philadelphians are committing a crime because they are driving without the legally required auto insurance (Joint Economic Committee 1996, 9).

Low-income Philadelphians are not the only urban motorists facing exorbitant costs. In South-Central Los Angeles, for example, the average annual per capita income is $7,000 while minimum liability coverage costs about $2,000. The city-council representative observes: "It's a function of putting food on the table versus paying for car insurance" (Joint Economic Committee 1998, 17). Given these choices, the decision of many urban and low-income drivers to break the law and become uninsured drivers can be one of good economic sense.

Uninsured motorists are a growing national problem. Some areas in Los Angeles and San Diego, for example, are estimated by the JEC to have uninsured-motorist rates of over 90 percent. These high rates turn the tort system into a crapshoot. An accident with one of these drivers means that you will receive nothing from insurance and collect, if awarded a judgment, only from their limited or nonexistent assets.

The uninsured-motorist problem feeds itself. Two economists (Smith and Wright 1992) ask "Why Is Automobile Insurance in Philadelphia So Damn Expensive?" Their answer is "that the high price of auto insurance can be attributed at least in part to the large number of uninsured drivers in some localities, while at the same time, the large number of uninsured motorists can be attributed at least in part to high premiums" (p. 759). In other words, premiums rise as more people pay nothing into the insurance pool while retaining their rights to claim from it. This direct correlation highlights the need to find systematic savings that make insurance more affordable and thereby enlarge the number of contributors to the insurance pool.

The growing number of uninsured drivers—over five million in California alone—is particularly bad news because it is the riskiest drivers (with the highest insurance rates) who are most likely to forego insurance. Thus, the rate of accident-prone drivers who are on the highways uninsured is perhaps as high as 50 percent (Tobias 1997, 84). This high percentage turns the insurance crapshoot into a fixed game of chance—the odds of being injured by an uninsured driver are exceedingly high.

High Costs and Cities

The decay of American cities is inextricably intertwined with automobiles. The rise of the auto (and the resulting fall of the trolley, bus, and train) helped isolate many urban residents. This link is explored by Jon C. Teaford (1990) in *The Rough Road to Renaissance: Urban Revitalization in America, 1940–1985*, which concludes that "[c]hanges in transportation and the advent of an automobile-dependent culture posed one of the most serious challenges to the central cities" (p. 5). Inner-city residents were left behind as the middle class drove off to new lives.

Automobiles now plague cities in the form of exorbitant insurance costs. Consider, for example, that the average annual premium charged in 1994 by State Farm for minimum liability coverage in Los Angeles was $811, while identical coverage in nearby suburban Northridge was less than $600 (O'Connell, Abrahamse, and Vaiana 1995, 291–92). This rate differential is a carrot for fleeing cities. Residents moving to the suburbs know that the difference of a few miles can give them the equivalent of a large tax cut—a significant premium savings. How can we expect more Americans to live and work in our cities when we also make it extraordinarily expensive to live there?

Workers who stay behind face a limited job market further constricted by the lack of reliable mobility. Waller and Hughes (1999) have explained public transit's limited ability to connect the poor to entry-level jobs that fall outside the 9-to-5 week. Other studies show that welfare recipients who own a car are 12 percent more likely to work, work an additional twenty-three hours per month, and bring home an additional $152 a month (Joint Economic Committee 1998, 22a). How can we expect welfare mothers to go to work when it costs them more than a thousand dollars to put a car on the road?

Perhaps the most insidious effect of the current system on city life (and also the most overlooked) is its undermining of civil society. James Q. Wilson, the eminent social scientist, teaches that "fixing windows" prevents urban life from deteriorating (Cohen 1999, 25). The theory is simple yet elegant: An unrepaired window leads to other windows being broken. At its heart is the notion that paying attention to small things—fare beating and vandalism, for example—has a disproportionate effect on big things. "If the neighborhood cannot keep a bothersome panhandler from annoying pass-ersby, the thief may reason, it is even less likely to call the police to identify a potential mugger or to interfere if the mugging actually takes place" (Wilson 1991, 130).

Wilson has received the rarest honor bestowed on a social scientist: His ideas are being acted upon. Many experts credit Wilson's broken-windows theory for the recent reduction of crime in New York and other cities (Bernstein 1998). When nuisance crimes are targeted, Wilson's theory of crime prevention is being put into place.

The relationship between broken windows and automobile insurance should be evident. We have already seen how high tort costs cause Philadelphians and other urban motorists to drive uninsured, to select between employment and illegality. The present system is coercing other-wise law-abiding Americans to act illegally. It is thereby planting the seed of illegality in inner cities across the country. The system is a broken window yet to be fixed. How can urban communities set high standards when most residents are violating the law every time they get behind the wheel?

High Costs and the Poor

To be sure, all drivers—rich and poor—may legitimately complain about the present insurance system. But low-income drivers have special complaints that highlight the current inequity.

Most obviously, the tort system operates like a regressive tax on the law-abiding poor. In his unpublished 1993 study of Maricopa County, Arizona, Robert Maril of Oklahoma State University found that 50.9 percent of low-income residents put off paying other important expenses to meet

TABLE 3. Auto Insurance Cost as a Share of Household Income

Income	Percent
Lowest fifth	16.3
Second	7.3
Third	4.4
Fourth	3.3
Highest fifth	2.3

Source: Horowitz 1998, 1.

insurance costs. Of these individuals, 44.1 percent reported deferring food purchases to pay for car insurance. The low-income residents of Maricopa County are not alone. Nationwide, as Table 3 indicates, households in the bottom fifth of income average pay 16.3 percent of their income for car insurance.

Even worse, these drivers are straining their budgets to pay for a product—liability insurance—that offers them little. Low-income drivers receive few benefits in exchange for high premiums because they have few assets to protect (and, like everyone else, they receive nothing in single-car accidents or accidents where they are deemed at "fault").

Moreover, tort forces the poor to pay disproportionately large amounts while simultaneously withholding its generosity. The poor pay and pay, but rarely fully collect. When low-income drivers do sue, their economic recovery is relatively small because jury verdicts typically reproduce the distribution of wealth. The lower your pre-accident salary, the lower your award. And worse, this reduced figure also causes the poor to receive less for their "pain and suffering" since this noneconomic recovery is calculated as a multiple of economic loss. In the eyes of tort, the pain of, say, a fast-food server is not as valuable as an executive's.

These biases are an indelible feature of the fault system; *by design* tort forces low-income drivers to subsidize BMW owners. This inequity exists because the third-party system pays an unknown individual whose losses cannot be predicted in advance. Since premiums must be based on compensation costs for "average" claimants, and cannot be crafted for specific individuals, low-income drivers (by definition below "average") foot the bill for higher-income drivers.

Tort law in action has yet another regressive feature: It disadvantages victims unable to wait out a protracted legal settlement. These claimants often accept a less than optimal settlement because their need for immediate payment outweighs their desire for a higher payment. "[T]he negotiated settlement rewards the sophisticated claimant and penalizes the inexperienced, the naïve, the simple, and the indifferent," observes a prominent sociologist. "I believe that the settlement produces relatively more for the affluent, the white, and the city dweller. It penalizes the poor, the uneducated, the [African-American and the rural dweller] . . ." (Ross 1980, 241–42).

High Costs and Government

The interplay between tort law and auto accidents diverts large amounts of tax revenue away from meaningful pursuits of statecraft (Joint Economic Committee 1998). Most directly, state and local governments must use public funds to insure their 3.3 million vehicles. These vehicles further drain public funds when they are the source of auto-tort claims, which are the most common lawsuits brought against government. And because of the perception of government having "deep pockets," jurors are less reluctant to award large verdicts in these cases. According to a 1995 survey cited by the JEC, the government (state and federal) was the defendant in 29 percent of all jury verdicts exceeding $1 million even though verdicts this size are less than 8 percent of all verdicts.

Taxpayers end up paying even when government is not a party because administrative costs must rise to handle the auto-accident litigation. According to the JEC, these cases account for 60 percent of the tort docket in the nation's seventy-five most populous counties. This deluge of tort filings also carries a nonmonetary cost—justice delayed is often justice denied. Because judges can hear only one case at a time, worthy nonautomobile claims stagnate.

High Costs and Business

As the Joint Economic Committee (1998) further documents, the private sector also ends up paying for the fault system. Expensive liability insurance is a drag on the economy. A survey of twelve industrialized nations found that these costs consume about 1.24 percent of our gross domestic product, about twice the average of the other eleven countries and three times the rate of England or Japan. Overall, in 1994, U.S. businesses spent $21 *billion* on auto liability insurance—an average of more than $64,000 per on-the-job automobile injury.

But companies had best not skimp on this insurance: Auto-accident lawsuits are the most common claims filed against businesses. These claims hamper all businesses, particularly small or growing enterprises. One example documented by the JEC is "Kids on the Go," a child-transport system founded in 1994. The mother-owner had to shut down her fledgling business after less than a year because the annual premium for two vans and four drivers was almost $14,000.

"Kids on the Go" is not the only transportation business to be a no go. Most of these companies, per the JEC, spend up to $6,000 per vehicle on liability insurance—a steep amount especially when you consider that that almost one-half (44 percent) of the vehicles generate only $10,000 in gross revenue annually. With these vehicles, liability costs alone eat up 60 percent of the gross revenue.

"In America, there are three ways to get rich. You can work hard (but that's no fun). You can win the lottery (perfect—except for the long odds). Or you can get in a car wreck and sue" (Spiro and Mirvish 1989, 24). But we have seen that, like tarnished brass, the tort system has less shine than expected upon closer inspection. Too many receive little or nothing for their injuries and everyone else pays too much. But Americans are optimists. The next section shows that many of us still take to heart those bumper stickers saying, "All You Need is an Accident and a Dream."

☐ 4. THE LURE OF LITIGATION

> Litigation, n. A machine which you go into as a pig and come out of as a sausage.—*Ambrose Bierce*

Airbags, antilock brakes, and campaigns against drunk driving are recent technological advances and public policy initiatives intended to make driving safer. Common sense says these measures have reduced accidents—an intuition that proves to be true. Accidents have become less frequent and less serious. Today, the traffic fatality rate in the United States is bested by only Great Britain and Sweden—1.8 deaths for every 100 million miles of vehicle travel (Johnston 1997, 188).

Of course, with fewer accidents, there should also be fewer lawsuits. But the opposite is true: Accidents and tort filings are moving in opposite directions. Driving has never been safer and yet there are more lawsuits than ever. While property claims declined 12 percent in the 1980s, bodily injury claims rose 15 percent (Insurance Research Council 1990). Nationally, the ratio of bodily injury claims per 100 property-damage claims went from 17.9 in 1980 to 29.5 in 1995 (Insurance Research Council 1996b).

Specific examples illustrate the litigiousness. In New York, for example, the number of bodily injury accidents decreased from 220,000 (in 1988) to 190,000 (in 1996) during a decade that witnessed 19,000 *more* lawsuits. In Washington, D.C., the number of lawsuits arising from auto accidents increased 137 percent between 1985 and 1995, even though the number of accidents fell 22 percent (Nguyen 1996). This trend can be seen across the country.

Anecdotal evidence also shows the growth business of litigation. Take, for example, the travails of my friend Randy. She was in a minor fender bender in D.C. where, instead of simply trading information and moving on, the other driver insisted on waiting for the police. So, they stood on the side of the road chatting (and laughing) for nearly three hours. When the police finally arrived, the officers said a formal report was unnecessary because the cars were drivable (one had a minor dent) and no one was injured. At that moment, the other driver announced for the first time, "I think my head and back hurt." Irate at this obvious lie, the police called for an ambulance. Unsurprisingly, the man refused treatment, sending the ambulance back to the hospital without him. Randy's insurance company, nonetheless, later settled the man's bodily injury claims for nearly $8,000.

The legitimacy of these claims against Randy and others is called into question by a striking dichotomy: the claim-rate contrast between rural and urban areas. Though rural drivers generally suffer greater injuries because of higher speeds, the increasing percentage of bodily injury claims as a percentage of all accidents is concentrated in cities. To use Pennsylvania as an example, for every 100 property-damage claims, there are 13 bodily injury claims in Harrisburg, 16 in Pittsburgh, and 75 in Philadelphia (Insurance Research Council 1990, 17–18). Brotherly love seems to be in short supply.

Table 4 illustrates this different claiming behavior in ten cities and states with data on the rate of bodily injury claims per 100 accidents (with accidents being measured as the number of property-damage claims). Simply put, this measure tells us how often people claim to be injured in accidents. In California, for example, outside of Los Angeles there are about forty-five bodily injury claims for every 100 accidents, that is, people are claiming to be injured in about half of all accidents. But look at Los Angeles: The injury rate is more than double (ninety-nine bodily injury claims per 100 accidents). That number is spectacular and worth emphasizing: Only *one LA resident in a hundred* is not filing a claim for personal injury after their car is involved in an accident.

The cities listed in Table 4 have different legal environments, insurance systems, populations, crime rates, and so on. City-by-city comparisons are thus difficult—is Memphis really like Newark?—but one trend is consistent: Claiming frequency is higher in cities than in the rest of the state.[5]

TABLE 4. Number of Bodily Injury Claims per 100 Property-Damage Claims in Selected Cities Compared to Rest of State

	City	Rest of State	Ratio
Los Angeles, CA	98.8	44.5	2:22
Newark, NJ	79.6	32.8	2:42
Philadelphia, PA	78.5	22.4	3:50
Baltimore, MD	62.1	36.6	1:69
Charlotte, NC	58.1	41.8	1:39
Milwaukee, WI	43.9	29.4	1:49
Cleveland, OH	40.8	28.5	1:43
Memphis, TN	35.7	25.3	1:41
Miami, FL	29.4	18.2	1:62
New York, NY	27.6	10.3	2:67

Source: Joint Economic Committee 1998, 8.

How to explain this anomaly of rising claims, decreasing accidents? The answer is not de-evolution. We may lack the robustness of Lewis and Clark, but surely we are not more vulnerable than our grandparents to fender benders. No, Americans are instead suing more and more because the tort system lures many accident "victims" (and their lawyers) to seek easy money. Thus, to the toll of physical injury caused by accidents is added a toll of encouraged exaggeration. These two tolls ultimately have a high cost: the distorted compensation and exorbitant expenditures discussed in the previous section.

This section focuses on the expensive cycle of litigation underlying the fault system. The temptations of large payoffs are first explored. The possibility of receiving unearned money for accidents—of mining fortune from misfortune—makes the tort system resemble Eden's apple: Every day Americans take a bite. The section then inspects the ultimate cause of the system's high costs and inefficiencies: the (too) prominent role of lawyers.

Tort's Temptations

In 1991, two thousand Americans were asked: "What are you honestly willing to do for $10 million?" The results are illuminating. Twenty-five percent would abandon their entire family; 23 percent would become prostitutes for a week or more; 10 percent would withhold testimony and let a murderer go free; 7 percent would kill a stranger; 4 percent would have a sex-change operation; and 3 percent would put their children up for adoption (Perlmutter 1997, 75).

Greed can also be seen in lawsuits. As in other areas of life, the higher the stakes, the greater the temptation to succumb to dishonesty. And make no mistake: The stakes in accident litigation may be less than $10 million, but they can be very tempting.

This temptation helps explain why a 1992 study of 15,000 auto-accident insurance claims in nine states found that about 36 percent of all bodily injury claims appeared to involve padding or outright fraud (Insurance Research Council 1996a, 1–3). One in three! As a result, the authors estimated that excess injury payments are between 17 percent and 20 percent of total paid losses, or $5.2 to $6.3 billion additional for all injury claims.

"The fact that tort-based auto insurance is third party creates a fertile environment for one of society's most costly and pervasive white-collar crimes: insurance fraud" (Detlefsen 1998, 5). Investigations indicate that some of this fraud is in the form of fake claims—phony claims, staged accidents, and jump-ins—often orchestrated by lawyers and doctors. But more common is claim exaggeration intended to obtain larger settlements from the other driver's insurance company (Bell and O'Connell 1997, 163). Both types merit discussion. We will explore padding first (inflating claims) and then turn to organized fraud (manufacturing claims).

Inflating Claims

Is padding an insurance claim a crime or not? Increasingly, Americans seem to believe the latter. Twenty-eight percent of drivers, according to a survey conducted by the Insurance Research Council (IRC; 1995), believe that padding is appropriate to recover a deductible, and 24 percent think that it is appropriate to make up for past premiums. From 1981 to 1995, 19 percent to 31 percent of those responding—depending on the year—informed the IRC that it was appropriate to falsify an insurance claim to make up for a deductible or previous premiums. Moreover, to inflate a claim, a significant percentage approved of unnecessary medical treatment (11 percent) or allowing a doctor to submit medical bills for treatment not received (8 percent).

Everyone pays for this lax attitude. Claim padding "sets a vicious cycle in motion: Insurance companies continue to increase premiums for the entire pool of insureds to cover the higher losses, while some consumers file for additional uncovered amounts to make up for the higher premiums charged" (Emerson 1992, 916). In 1995, the Federal Bureau of Investigation estimated that "[e]very American household is burdened with over $200 annually in additional premiums to make up for this type of fraud" (Joint Economic Committee 1998, 2).

Social acceptance of padding will not go away. This attitude will continue to prevail—and even increase—with a certain portion of the population. Overstated and false claims will add costs to any auto-insurance system; fraud is a fact of life. But a fundamental problem with the fault system is that it adds fuel to the fire by promising windfall payments and money for nonmonetary losses.

Easy Money   The additional automobile claims of recent years mostly constitute claims for "soft-tissue" injuries such as sprains and whiplash (Insurance Research Council 1994, 21). Not coincidentally, these injuries are also the most difficult to diagnose. At the same time there has been a drop in the number of objectively diagnosable "hard" injuries such as broken bones.

Tort awards are a magnet for these soft-tissue claims. By adding these allegations, claimants (and their lawyers) in no-fault states seek to inflate their claim value above threshold limits and thereby "double dip" from no-fault and fault benefits. And, in tort states, claimants seek to maximize their potential litigation recovery from the other party.

The magnetic pull of potential tort awards is seen in the ratio of soft-tissue injuries to hard injuries in states with the fault system. In California, for instance, auto-accident victims claim about 250 soft-tissue injuries for every 100 hard injuries (Carroll, Abrahamse, and Vaiana 1995, 23). On the other hand, in Michigan, which has the country's strongest no-fault scheme, the ratio is 70 to 100. Are Michiganders more resilient than Californians? No. It is simply that they have less incentive to run up medical bills.

With no limits on lawsuits, Californians also have more reasons to hire a lawyer after an accident, and do so twice as often as Michigan residents—40.2 percent versus 20.5 percent, respectively (Sprinkel 1988, 19). A certain naiveté is required to believe there is no relationship between the higher rate of attorney involvement and the higher ratio of whiplash claims.

Thresholds, as we have seen, arose from no-fault proposals being gutted by tort advocates. Time has shown that these political compromises, particularly the monetary thresholds, fail to exclude minor cases from the tort system. They instead set a target at which victims and lawyers aim. As one lawyer puts it: "Keep taking X-rays until you jump the threshold or you glow in the dark" (Bedard 1998).

Hawaii and Massachusetts are case studies on the failure of monetary thresholds. In Hawaii, where the threshold was $7,000 in 1990, the median number of visits for claimants seeing chiropractors was fifty-eight per claimed injury; one-quarter of the claimants made more than eighty-four visits (Insurance Research Council 1996a, 26). Similarly, when Massachusetts raised its threshold from $500 to $2,000, the median number of claims-related medical treatment visits per claimant more than doubled (Marter and Weisberg 1992, 488). Not coincidentally, in 1995, a Boston chiropractor convicted of insurance fraud required patients to make at least twenty-five visits and receive at least $2,000 worth of treatments (Joint Economic Committee 1998, 14).

Given these perverse incentives—another Massachusetts doctor's yacht is called "Whiplash"—some advocate widespread adoption of the descriptive thresholds used in Florida, Michigan, and New York. But this suggestion overlooks the failure of verbal thresholds to deal effectively with larger tort claims. Studies show that the tort claims preserved over verbal thresholds contribute disproportionately to total personal-injury costs (O'Connell, Carroll, Horowitz, and Abrahamse 1993, 1019). Besides, as we have seen, lawyers in these states are increasingly adept at scaling even these thresholds.

The tort system, through claims for negligence, allows and even encourages people to view accidents as investment opportunities. The lure of easy money is so strong that auto insurance must end its relationship with this lottery system—a lottery that you win by wringing out a settlement bigger than your costs. Thresholds are not a divorce or even a trial separation; claimants in every state continue to file suit. But first-party insurance similar to home and life coverage would, finally, break the link between accident compensation and litigation.

Pain and Suffering   A trial lawyer uses the closing argument to ask for money in three categories: medical expenses (to date and future), wage loss (to date and future), and pain and suffering (to date and future). The jury then deliberates and fills in the six blank lines.

The amount of medical expenses and wage losses (together, "economic damages") are generally straightforward. But the third category—noneconomic damages—defies calculator computation. "Pain and suffering" is the catchall term for these subjective reactions to an accident. The key factor is that physiological pain, emotional distress, and other nonpecuniary losses are wholly subjective. W. Kip Viscusi of Harvard Law School (1996, 169) explains: "[J]uries currently do not have precise quantitative guidance. They are asked to apply their 'enlightened conscience' to assess a value for pain and suffering compensation." Similarly, a Michigan federal court, in *Donahoo v. Turner Construction Company* (833 F. Supp.

621, 623 (E.D. Mich. 1993)), concluded, "The law . . . dictates no method of calculating pain and suffering damages."

Economic and noneconomic damages are intertwined. Awards for pain and suffering increase in correlation to the amount of wage loss and medical expenses; they are multiples of actual damages. As observed by Cornell University's Charles W. Wolfram (1986, 528): "Pain and suffering and similar nonmonetary damages probably average three times the monetary damages in personal injury claims." In automobile cases, the data indicate that the operative ratios are $2.11 in pain and suffering for every dollar of medical and wage loss costs and $3.00 in pain and suffering for every dollar of medical cost alone (Brickman 1994, 1782).

Even armchair psychologists can see that this provides an incentive for patients (and their lawyers and doctors) to maximize medical bills. Every extra treatment adds to the pot of money available. This potential payoff does not inspire conservative care—it is a call to go overboard. Too often the treatment is not legitimate.

The wholly subjective nature of pain and suffering is leverage for boosting claim value. This idea is expressed with élan by Douglas LaFaive in *The Claims Game* (1991), which helps accident victims appraise their claims. LaFaive observes: "Pain and suffering are very subjective elements of your claim. . . . Who is to say that one person hurts, or feels pain, more than another person? The answer is: No one can!" (p. 36) But seeming impossibility does not discourage the author. Instead, LaFaive crafts a "multiplier factor," which essentially multiplies the amount of hospital bills by five, and a "pain-and-suffering factor," which estimates these damages alone to be worth $500 a month (pp. 35–37). Which is superior? It depends on which offers the highest claim value, as is seen in LaFaive's hypothetical scenario where economic damages (medical bills and wage loss) are $1,467:

> Using the Multiplier Factor yields an estimated settlement value of $2,887.00 or $1,420.00 for pain and suffering. In all probability, the injured would consider this to be an unacceptably low settlement value and a settlement would be resisted.
>
> Using the Pain and Suffering Factor, on the other hand, yields an estimated settlement value of $4,467.00 or $3,000.00 for pain and suffering. This settlement value is much more in line with the average claim (p. 43).

LaFaive is not alone in devising "factors" for learning the un-learnable—most lawyers and claims adjusters have pet theories for deter-mining the value of pain and suffering. But his book underscores that noneconomic damages are wildcards. Operating with vague instructions and insufficient standards, juries can open the pocketbooks of others. Consider the following 1990 case selected almost at random from a published collection of verdicts from across the country (Jury Verdict Research, Inc. 1993, 26–27).

A Portland man filed suit after his car collided with the defendant's turning trailer. He alleged that one physical injury—a strained neck and back—caused, among other things, posttraumatic stress disorder, adjustment disorder, panic disorder, agoraphobia, chronic anxiety, depression, fear of driving, and morbid thoughts. The jury awarded him $18,600—$5,615 for economic damages and $12,385 for pain and suffering. (The judge reduced the verdict to $9,300 because the plaintiff was found to be 50-percent negligent.)

In this case noneconomic damages were almost two-thirds (65 percent) of the total verdict. This pattern of larger awards for intangible losses than for actual losses is repeated every day. You should not be surprised, then, to learn that noneconomic damages are popular with plaintiffs' attorneys. In fact, the ability to generate large pain-and-suffering awards is what distinguishes star trial lawyers. Any competent attorney can show the jury how much was spent in medical bills and lost in wages. But only the gifted few can make jurors really feel every twinge of the plaintiff's pain.

Trial lawyers understand that jury empathy and verdict size go hand in hand. The creation of a sympathetic client is the overarching goal for everything from jury selection to closing argument. One tactic is the use of analogies and metaphors. An example: "The scar on John's face may be minimal to the defense, but not to John. A small tear in a Van Gogh painting will destroy the value of that piece of art. Why should John be treated any differently?" (Rundlett 1991, 47)

Another common tactic is to market pain and suffering as a markup over medical bills and lost wages. Because you may never have seen a trial (watching *L.A. Law* does not count), here is part of a closing argument praised in an ATLA-published article entitled "The Psychology of the Large Award":

> So, the question is, what in justice's name is the sum which is necessary to compensate for all that has happened up to now, for what faces him the future for the rest of his years? Three years past; twenty-two years of future. Of course, the amount gets large. . . . [W]e say if $75 a day were allowed for what is past, for what he went through, and for what he has to face for all the years, that is $600,000, $630,000. How do you figure it (Landau 1979, 75)?

Yes, a Hollywood screenwriter could probably draft something more dramatic. But the important thing is that these tactics actually work—they sway jurors. As we have seen, juries in automobile cases typically award over two dollars in pain and suffering for every dollar of medical and wage loss and three dollars in pain and suffering for every dollar of medical cost alone. Unfortunately, these payments raise the cost of liability insurance (not to mention health-care costs generally) and create perverse litigation incentives.

If physical harm is so severe as to cause disability, the disability should be compensated (as are physical injuries) for its economic consequences. Intangible harm alone should not be compensated by auto insurance. "Despite propaganda campaigns by trial lawyers' associations seeking to convince the public that pain and suffering damages are the inalienable birthright of every freedom-loving American," notes Richard Abel (1990, 823), "surveys of victims demonstrate repeatedly that they do not want it. . . . Nonpecuniary damages also dehumanize the response to misfortune, substituting money for compassion, arousing jealousy instead of sympathy, and treating experience and love as commodities."

Pain-and-suffering awards are an incentive for fraud unique to liability insurance. No one has a health-insurance policy for the pain of an operation or a home-insurance policy for the anguish of his or her house burning down. Thus, removing pain-and-suffering damages from automobile insurance would not only eliminate an inducement for padding, it would also bring the system into line with other insurance policies owned by Americans.

Manufacturing Claims

Fraud covers the spectrum from ingenuity to opportunism (Fitzgerald 1999, 2–3). For example, in so-called "phony claims," neither the accident nor the injury is real. Someone instead obtains a damaged vehicle and a tractor-trailer's license number and then sends the trucking company a phony accident report and photograph claiming that the car was forced off the road.

In staged accidents, little or no real injury results. An example:

[T]he most popular staged accident is the "swoop and squat" maneuver, which involves a minimum of three vehicles. The target vehicle [often driven by a mother distracted by children] . . . is spotted along a multilane highway. The "swoop" vehicle makes a lane change in front of the cooperating "squat" car. The squat car then stops suddenly in front of the following target vehicle. Often a fourth vehicle, also part of the team, rides alongside the target vehicle to prevent a lane change. The resulting accident is the "fault" of the driver of the target vehicle, and the multiple occupants of the squat car (carefully belted) once again file phony and inflated claims (Bell and O'Connell 1997, 163–64).

In jump-ins, the accident may be real but the injury is not. For example, in 1993, a bus waiting at a New Jersey stoplight was rear-ended by a slow-moving car. The fifteen "passengers" on the bus were actually state investigators who watched seventeen people hop on *after* the accident (but before the police arrived) and later describe their "injuries" to police officers. Eventually 107 people, including lawyers and medical practitioners, were charged with insurance fraud (Joint Economic Committee 1998, 13–14).

Attorneys and physicians are often the masterminds behind fraudulent attempts to cash in on crashes. In a memorable 1980 investigation conducted by the *Chicago Sun-Times* and WLS-TV, reporters showed how the automobile-insurance swindle allows the client, the lawyer, and the doctor to all benefit. "This is all just a jigsaw puzzle," said one practicing personal-injury lawyer to the reporters. "When all the pieces fit together, it spells money" (Zekman and Mustain 1980, 6–7).

To be sure, faked personal injuries have a rich history in America. Since the late nineteenth century, fraud has been a part of the real-world operation of insurance. As Ken Dornstein documents in *Accidentally, On Purpose* (1996, 240), there is "a deep American impulse to make a market in anything (even fake accidents) in order to get ahead." But this "impulse" is granted free reign by a tort system that pays claimants. A true no-fault system would make these incentives to cash in disappear—and, along with them, much of the fraud bedeviling the country.

The Role of Lawyers

The fundamental flaw with the current system is that lawyers control it. As Andrew Tobias testified before the Senate's Commerce Committee:

> [T]oday's $7-an-hour worker, if he obeys the law in most states, is forced to buy insurance that pays lawyers $125-an-hour to fight his claim, if he's hurt, and that then typically requires him to give up 33% or 40% plus expenses of anything he wins to the lawyer who helped him win it (Joint Economic Committee 1998, 32).

Lawyers love car-accident litigation because there is so much of it. Nationally, these cases represent three-quarters of all fees collected in personal-injury lawsuits (Hensler et al. 1991, 101). But the popularity of books and movies about lawsuits obscures the fact that personal-injury litigation can be an expensive, time-consuming, and zero-sum game. The wisdom of Abraham Lincoln was probably never more evident than when he exhorted lawyers:

> Discourage litigation. Persuade your neighbors to compromise whenever you can. Point out to them how the nominal winner is often a real loser—in fees, expenses, and waste of time. As a peacemaker the lawyer has a superior opportunity to be a good man. There will still be business enough (Glendon 1994, 55).

Perhaps the strongest indictment of the present system is that it does not follow the teaching of Lincoln.[6]

Is a Million Lawyers Enough? Part of the disturbing litigation trend—more claims, less accidents—must be related to the proliferation of attorneys. Many of these lawyers want (and need) to turn auto accidents into financial gain. *E miseria res secundae*: out of misery, prosperity.

For the century after the Civil War, the growth rate of lawyers mirrored that of the general population. Since 1970, however, the profession has exhibited rabbit-like tendencies: The current ratio of one lawyer to every three hundred laypersons is double its historical average. There are already more than 850,000 lawyers in the United States and thousands of new ones are produced each year (Lasson 1994, 730–31).[7]

All of these lawyers need to earn a living; supply pushes demand. As a Seton Hall law professor notes, "The large number of cases filed and the vastly increased number of attorneys admitted to practice may be coincidental, but economic necessity on the attorneys' part at least suggests a causal relationship" (Kerekes 1994, 492).

Certainly, civil lawyers draft wills, help with taxes, and so on, but many are involved with personal-injury litigation. As Stanford University's Lawrence Friedman (1985, 684) notes: "Since the 1920s, the automobile has played a larger and larger role in everyday tort law. Practically speaking, most personal-injury lawyers work on auto-accident cases. . . . The automobile accident is the bread and butter of tort law." It is no wonder, then, that Friedman notes: "[N]o-fault makes steady progress, though over the dead bodies (so to speak) of personal injury lawyers."

Looking for a Good Lawyer? Anyone who has scanned the Yellow Pages or watched television knows that personal-injury lawyers advertise widely and aggressively. But it may surprise some readers to learn that this advertising is a recent phenomenon. In the not-too-distant past, lawyers were prohibited from advertising their services. In 1977, however, in the name of the First Amendment, the Supreme Court held that a state may not prohibit advertising about the availability and cost of legal services (Glendon 1994, 54–55). The result? A flood of attorney commercials, billboards, and toll-free hotlines. A perusal of Washington, D.C.'s phone book, for example, reveals dozens of law firms offering the same promise: "Injured? We can help."

Attorneys would not spend all this time and money on ineffectual advertising. It is therefore doing one of two things. The commercials either increase the number of litigants or give law firms a larger slice of a static pool of claimants. I suspect the first is true; it seems reasonable that some (many?) people file suit because they are deluged with lawyers promoting a free service.[8] If so, then the commercials promote lawsuits, which add costs to each claim, which cause premiums to rise. This circle of expensive litigiousness can only be broken by changing the system—by minimizing the role of lawyers.

No Recovery, No Fee?   Although advertising is important, the contingency fee is the motor that drives accident litigation. Indeed, as my informal review confirms, almost every Yellow-Pages listing stresses the "no-recovery-no-fee" theme.

A contingency fee is one where a lawyer is paid only from money actually recovered in the lawsuit. The arrangement raises visceral emotions. Some see it as providing a key to the courthouse, and others as unleashing suit-happy litigators. But my goal is not to pick sides; it is to comment on observed facts about accidents and contingency fees.

As a preliminary matter, it should be noted that contingency fees are almost universal in accident claims. Ninety-five percent of personal-injury representations are contingent-fee arrangements and 97 percent of attorneys accept personal-injury cases *only* on a contingent basis ("Settling for Less" 1993, 448). Practically speaking, then, an accident victim wanting to enter the tort system with a lawyer as a Sherpa will have to sign a contingency-fee retainer.

With the millions of these agreements extant, you would expect there to be a range of rates. Not so. The amounts charged are remarkably inelastic (Brickman, Horowitz, and O'Connell 1994). Accident victims are almost always charged one-third of the recovery—sometimes more, rarely less.[9] "[O]ne can drop into just about any American city or town, knowing ahead of time that death and taxes are not the only things that can be counted on with certainty," notes a San Francisco lawyer (Kennedy 1981). "In addition to being able to find a Coke and a Big Mac, one also knows that when purchasing a house, the real-estate broker's commission will almost certainly be 6 percent and, if one is injured, the lawyer's contingent fee will be at least 33–1/3 percent."

This standard rate can translate into substantial sums of money, more than attorneys could charge a client paying an hourly rate. The traditional justification for these large payments is that lawyers receive a "risk premium" for the possibility that that they will not receive any payment for their services. (The common sense of this is exemplified in the adage "A bird in the hand is worth two in the bush.") But all too often this is a fiction. In truth, there is often little risk of no recovery. As a senior federal judge (Grady 1976, 24) has observed: "The vast majority of personal injury cases involve no uncertainty that the lawyer is going to be paid something. The only question is how much."

No critique of the present system is possible without acknowledging that contingency fees are universal, standard, and substantial. The present role of lawyers—and thus the method of paying them—is simply too much a part of the fault system to ignore. (After all, a primary objective of no fault is limiting the role of attorneys.) These facts lead to the following conclusions:

Many accident victims are being overcharged. Too often trial lawyers exploit their monopoly of access to the courts rather than their legal training. A Harvard-educated attorney is not needed to obtain a reasonable offer if a drunk driver rear-ends someone at a red light. But these clients with slam-dunk claims are being taxed at least one-third of the recovery even though there is little risk of nonpayment. This tax limits the available compensation and raises the costs for everyone else.

Lawyers are shortchanging some accident victims. Because lawyers assess their rate of return on a per-hour basis, the interests of client and lawyer diverge when a good-but-not-optimal settlement can be negotiated right out of the gate. If, say, a $5,000 settlement can be achieved after ten hours ($500 per hour), but a $10,000 one is likely after 100 hours ($100 per hour), it is in the lawyer's interest—but not the client's—to accept the $5,000 settlement. And, indeed, studies show that for recoveries under $10,000, contingent-fee lawyers devote significantly less time to their cases than do hourly fee lawyers (Brickman 1994, 1773).

Contingency fees promote exaggerated injuries. Contingency-fee lawyers have a financial incentive to inflate their clients' damages—the value of their percentage fee increases. A nationwide study of 46,694 auto claims paid during a two-week period in 1987 found that represented claimants, on average, incurred higher medical expenses (Brickman, Horowitz, and O'Connell 1994, 1783). Simply stated, contingency fees contribute to the billions of dollars spent each year on medical expenses, which are more important to claim value than patient health.

The widespread use of the contingency fee, in short, promotes litigation, taxes victim recovery, exposes claimants to a conflict of interest, and provides an incentive to inflate claims. The arrangement thus provides yet another reason to move away from liability theories as the primary source of compensating accident victims. Too many victims pay too many lawyers too much to do too little.

What Are Lawyers Worth? Lawyers are expensive. But are they worth it? Retaining a lawyer does not necessarily put you on the fast track to riches. When liability is not in doubt, a lawyer's services can be superfluous (Sullivan 1971, 101). One leading study found that while represented claimants often do obtain larger settlements, their net recoveries (after paying legal fees and litigation expenses) are often lower than those of nonrepresented claimants (Brickman, Horowitz, and O'Connell 1994, 31). For example, represented claimants with fractures incurred more than $4,800 in higher costs (mostly in increased medical expenses), to obtain, on average, $2,500 less in net payments.

More recently, the Insurance Research Council (1999) conducted a consumer panel survey of 5,768 persons who had been injured in the past three years in auto accidents. Forty percent of the respondents had retained attorneys to facilitate settlements. Less than half (46 percent) reported satisfaction with net settlement amounts, compared to almost three-quarters (73 percent) of claimants who did not hire attorneys. Represented claimants also netted fewer dollars, on average, than nonrepresented claimants. Nonrepresented claimants received a higher average net settlement of $832 in large measure because represented claimants paid an estimated 32 percent of their gross settlement in legal expenses.

These findings are not unique. The negative consequences of attorney retention were similarly observed in a study of New York's Workers' Compensation Program. "[C]laimants represented by attorneys obtained settlements that were significantly smaller than those obtained by nonrepresented claimants" (Thompson 1991, 221).

Besides being expensive, attorneys are also slow. Not every case resembles the endless litigation of *Jarndyce v. Jarndyce* in Dickens's *Bleak House*, but delays are endemic. A wait of sixteen months is not unusual. A result of this protracted legal skirmishing is that represented victims, on average, get paid more slowly than those who do not hire a lawyer. In one study, for example, a year after the auto insurer was notified of the accident, 95.4 percent of nonrepresented claimants had been paid, but 42.5 percent of represented ones were still awaiting compensation (Brickman, Horowitz, and O'Connell 1994, 36).

There are at least two unpleasant consequences to this delay. The first and most obvious is that accident victims do not get paid for an extended period. The second is that they are unable to get on with their lives. Meetings, depositions, and court appearances—all with the goal of showing permanent pain—mean reliving the accident for a year or more. No doctor would ever prescribe such a treatment regime. But lawyers do.

❑ 5. THE FAULTS OF FAULT

> I must say that as a litigant I should dread a lawsuit beyond almost anything else short of sickness and death.—*Judge Learned Hand*

Is the price of negligence too high? On this question turns much of the debate. An answer redeeming the central role of fault could, perhaps, tilt the balance in favor of litigation despite overwhelming evidence—high costs, unfairness, and fraud—of the system's shortcomings. But no such redemption is forthcoming.

Negligence is not one of the Ten Commandments. To the contrary, it is a secular tort, a product of the common law, which developed over time through court decisions and customs. It was to this organic nature that Oliver Wendell Holmes, Jr. referred when he began *The Common Law* (1881) by writing: "The life of the law has not been logic: it has been experience."

Although predating the Model T by more than two decades, this famous observation by the future Supreme Court justice is relevant to the current debate over no fault. Applying negligence theories to modern automobile accidents is not very logical, but it is done, in large part, because it was done in the past. The trouble is that the experience has been a poor one.

The Meaning of Negligence

Accidents predate negligence claims. The former have always existed; the latter are modern creations. From medieval times to about the middle of the nineteenth century, the primary rule of law was that "if a man is damaged he ought to be recompensed" (Mayer 1980, 233). That is, unlike negligence lawsuits, "liability was imposed, not because the defendant was at fault, but because the defendant caused the damage" (Lee and Lindahl 1994, 20). The defendant had the burden of showing himself to be utterly blameless for the damages.

As Holmes suggested, however, our legal system does not exist in a vacuum. Judges are not automatons; they reflect the social milieu. The New Deal of the 1930s and the civil rights movement of thirty years later both illustrate how political and social forces transform courthouses. This phenomenon was also visible, in spades, with the rise of industry and mass transportation. The Industrial Revolution brought extensive mechanization to industry and wrought an equally dramatic revolution in the courts.

Preindustrial accidents had been simple and rare compared to the by-product of the Industrial Revolution. (How much trouble could horses really get into?) But the technological advances of the late 1800s transformed America—and injured people in the process. In New York City, to look at the largest city, only thirteen personal-injury suits were brought in 1870. By 1910 that number had grown some 4,500 percent (Dornstein 1996, 224).

As personal-injury lawsuits became common, courts fretted over their potential for hampering economic growth. Judges feared that "[i]f railroads, and enterprise generally, had to pay for all damage done 'by accident,' lawsuits could drain them of their economic blood" (Friedman 1985, 468–69). These fears were real. "Safety first" was not the motto of the Industrial Revolution; there was no *Consumer Reports* or Occupational Safety and Health Administration. "Early railway trains, in particular, were notable neither for speed nor safety. They killed any object from a Minister of State to a wandering cow. . ." (Winfield 1926, 195).

To limit lawsuits, and to relax liability for accidents, courts seized upon the notion of "fault." "[N]egligence law was developed for the primary purpose of freeing infant enterprise of the 1800s from the burdens of tort liability imposed by the strict morality of earlier law" (Green 1958, 31). No longer would railroads and other defendants be liable for *all* the harms caused by their conduct; their liability would be limited to "negligent" conduct. Railroads were the immediate beneficiaries of this change; their injured passengers the losers.

The concept of negligence passed from Great Britain to the United States as each state (except Louisiana, which followed the civil code of France) adopted the new wrinkle to the common law (Kionka 1977, 23).

In the United States the necessity of proving negligence after an accident dates from around 1850 with the decision of the Massachusetts Supreme Court in *Brown v. Kendall* (60 Mass. 292, 6 Cush. 292 (1850)). We might say that *Brown* was the original tort reform.[10]

Although there have been important developments in negligence law, the precepts have remained largely the same since *Brown*: (1) Did the defendant owe a duty to the plaintiff? (2) Did the defendant breach that duty? (3) Did the breach cause the plaintiff's injuries? (4) Did the plaintiff, in fact, suffer harm? The plaintiff must get an affirmative response from the jury to each question—or, in legal parlance, "prove all four elements"—if she is to receive any compensation. In short, the four elements create the "tort of negligence." On the other hand, a person "is negligent" if he or she fails to live up to the second element of the negligence claim, breach of the standard of due care.

Negligence is commonly defined for juries as "the failure to do something which a reasonably careful person would do or the doing of something which a reasonably careful person would not do, under circumstances similar to those shown by the evidence" (Lee and Lindahl 1994, 21). Thus, and importantly, negligence does not track moral fault. Instead of examining the defendant's subjective intent, as the law does in murder prosecutions and other criminal trials, the jury in a negligence case must weigh the defendant's justifications in light of how an idealized abstraction—a "reasonable person"—would have acted ("Would a reasonable person have done (or not done) such-and-such?").[11]

A defendant can be found negligent even if personal shortcomings such as bad eyesight or poor hearing made it virtually impossible to meet the objective standard created by the "reasonable person" (Kionka 1977, 53). To impose legal fault for negligence on this individual is not to say that he or she "sinned" or is "morally wrong." Holmes made this point in another famous passage of *The Common Law*: "The standards of the law are standards of general application. The law takes no account of the infinite varieties of temperament, intellect, and education which make the internal character of a given act so different in different men" (p. 108).

Negligence and Cars

As we have seen, automobiles were absorbed into a legal system rooted in the common law. As a result, jurists viewed automobiles, and their inevitable accidents, through the prism of negligence (Hughes 1996). As in the aftermath of accidents involving carts and horses, courts asked a central question: Who is at fault?

This was the wrong query. With swift machines weighing tons apiece extracting a growing toll of injury and death, the question of "fault" was tangential. But like old generals refighting the last war, judges failed to appreciate the true extent of the social changes through which they were living. This blinkered vision was not limited to cars. "[T]he method of leisurely judicial adoption, case-by-case, was not well suited to many of the new problems generated by rapid urbanization and industrialization," notes Mary Ann Glendon (1994) of Harvard Law School. "Industrial accidents, for example, required thinking about aggregates rather than isolated instances; about long-range preventive planning as well as after-the-injury compensation" (p. 183). Slowly, sometimes too slowly, the legal system adapted to the new reality. "And, since its heyday in the late 19th century, [the fault principle] has been steadily eroded in area after area of the law" (O'Connell 1971, 125).

The story of the nineteenth century was saving U.S. business from being smothered by lawsuits. The twentieth century told a different tale—attention returned to the individual. The shifting paradigm is probably best seen in workers' compensation insurance, with its promise of compensation without regard to "fault." But the shifting of negligence law to meet new demands can also be seen elsewhere (James and Law 1952). The time has come to do the same with automobile accidents. The cars of today are the imaginary vehicles of which Jules Verne dreamt but they are governed by negligence laws founded on the horses and buggies that Verne rode.

Why Fault Is Faulty

The judicial instinct to allocate fault developed when technology was relatively unsophisticated and liability insurance was rare. The search for fault was rather simple, and a financial penalty awaited any defendant deemed negligent (Mooney 1989, 87). But these justifications—fault and fine—were true for only a limited period. That window closed long ago.

Congestion, high speeds, and other events all confuse and complicate the question of "fault." One example of surprise and speed confusing a passenger-witness occurred on 22 November 1963. Senator Ralph Yarborough, traveling behind President Kennedy's Dallas motorcade, told investigators that he smelled gunpowder—an impossibility, no matter who did the shooting—when he was sped away from Dealey Plaza (Posner 1994, 245).

The senator's confusion highlights that proof in auto-accident cases can be troubling and suspect, especially as speeds increase. "[E]vidence in automobile accident cases is particularly unreliable: Not only do litigants deliberately attempt to put their actions in the best light, but lack of attention is often a factor in automobile accidents from the very onset" (Dewees, Duff, and Trebilcock 1996, 41). The observations of the legendary tort scholar William Prosser (1964, 580) are worth quoting at length:

> The process by which the question of legal fault, and hence of liability, is determined in our courts is a cumbersome, time-consuming, expensive, and almost ridiculously inaccurate one. The evidence given in personal injury cases usually consists of highly contradictory statements from the two sides, estimating such factors as time, speed, distance and visibility, often months after the event by witnesses who were never very sure just what happened when they saw it, and whose faulty memories are undermined by lapse of time, by bias, by conversations with others, and by the subtle influence of counsel. Upon such evidence, a jury of twelve inexperienced citizens, called away from their other business if they have any, are invited to retire and make the best guess they can as to whether the defendant, the plaintiff, or both were "negligent". . . .

Many leading scholars agree with Prosser. "The problems of proof involved in automobile accident litigation under a negligence standard are so great that it is only the blindest of faith that permits hope in a large number of cases that what in fact occurred will become known," noted Cornelius Peck (1970, 64–65). "[I]t may be possible to say with confidence little more than that the parties were engaged in a particular activity—the use of motor vehicles."

Lawyers have long known the difficulties inherent to reconstructing an automobile accident in the courtroom. By "long known," I mean since at least the Depression and Franklin Roosevelt's first term. Here, for example, are future President Nixon's observations, published in 1936 during his last year of law school:

> In the days of poor roads and low speeds the facts of an accident could be reconstructed in a courtroom with some degree of accuracy, and the problem of determining fault did not present unusual difficulties. But with high-powered cars [!] and concrete highways, the probability that an accident—often the consequence of fractional mistake in management—can and will be described accurately in court has become increasingly remote, especially where court congestion has delayed the time of trial (p. 477).

A significant amount of judicial resources and professional effort are devoted every day to the mundane yet difficult question of what happened in fender benders. "Unhappily, the cases tried under the fault system tend to be those in which application of the fault criterion is most unrealistic. Cases in which the criterion can be realistically applied tend to be settled . . ." (Keeton 1969, 131).

Even if not futile, the pursuit of fault often lacks a moral dimension. Fatigue and poor vision, to name two accident-producing factors, cannot be called moral shortcomings. The hypothetical accident of section 1, for instance, did not involve a deliberate collision; the other driver no more wanted the accident than you. Yet for almost a year, time and money were spent exploring, at worst, a split-second judgment lapse.

Sometimes accidents are just accidents. Driving errors are nearly ubiquitous—an average driver may make a mistake as often as every two miles (Hager 1998, 803). The most comprehensive study of accident causation factors found that the driver was the sole factor in 57 percent of collisions and a contributing factor in 94 percent (Olson 1996, 5). But each failure to signal before changing lanes does not cause an accident. Many run-of-the-mill accidents instead occur when two drivers simultaneously make simple mistakes; there is an "act-of-God" randomness to these collisions (Ross 1980, 251).

What about the other reason for post-accident faultfinding—the possibility of penalty? This justification does not bear scrutiny very well, either. States have (wisely) undermined it by requiring drivers to carry liability insurance. As a result, a negligent driver pays for his or her sins, if at all, only in the form of higher future premiums. It is the insurance company, not the driver, which reaches into its pocket after the search for negligence is completed. Of course, truly irresponsible drivers who flout regulations or drive while intoxicated are punished by the criminal justice system. But these prosecutions will take place regardless of how insurance pays accident victims.

The two historical reasons for faultfinding are now history themselves. The tort system is ill equipped to blame one driver and pay the other. Criminal law and no-fault insurance, in conjunction, are better able to perform these two distinct tasks. This alone explains why the fault system needs to be overhauled.

Another reason is provided by a psychologist who looks at the tort system through the eyes of accident victims. "[T]he system encourages and, once invoked, perpetuates and quite probably deepens a conflict," notes Sally Lloyd-Bostock (1980, 345). "The data show how fault appears to be attributed because it can justify. . . . [T]he present system creates more hostility than it dispels. . . ."

Regardless, lawyers and other status-quo defenders cite the "failure" of no fault to engage in faultfinding as its fatal flaw. "Curtailing lawsuits will cause traffic accidents," the argument runs, "because drivers will not be checked by the fear of being sued." But this is a Potemkin village, all false fronts. It falls apart in at least four ways.

In the first place, and leaving aside the fact that unsafe motorists will always be exposed to higher premiums and criminal prosecutions, the same lawyers argue the opposite in other contexts. For instance, in products liability cases, the plaintiffs' bar is an eloquent opponent of the argument that misuse of a product (known as contributory negligence) should be a barrier to recovery in tort. Thus, the same trial lawyer seeking to file a products liability suit on behalf of a negligent client wants to prevent someone else who may be seen as "at fault" from receiving compensation for a road accident.

Also selectively applied is the argument that fault liability has a deterrent effect. Consider, for example, workers' compensation insurance (a "pure" no-fault law). I hear no one claiming that this universal insurance sacrifices safety and must be abandoned to reduce injury rates.

Third, the deterrence argument risks making a parody of tort law. The tort system, after all, save for exceptional cases where punitive damages are awarded, does not seek to punish wrongdoers so much as it seeks to compensate victims (Harper, James, and Gray 1986, 106). Damages paid to a victim via settlement or jury verdict are not commensurate with fault; the principal goal is reparation. The issue of whether the individual pays his or her "victim" is less important than the fact that the injured person is paid. The principal goal of the tort system is to deal with the welfare of accident victims. And tort is doing its job poorly.

Finally, the argument begs this question: Does the tort system actually deter unsafe driving? I doubt it. Drivers have plenty of incentives other than avoidance of lawsuits to avoid accidents. Do you attempt to drive safely so as to protect yourself and your passengers or to avoid a lawsuit? The answer, I submit, is obvious. And, in this case, the obvious answer is also correct. As Stephen Sugarman (1989) has documented, there are no studies effectively documenting that tort law affects the quality of driving. The federal government agrees. "No fault auto insurance laws do not lead to more accidents. . . . [T]he highway fatality and injury rate in no fault States exhibits no significant difference from those in traditional States" (U.S. Department of Transportation 1985, 6).

In point of fact, using the term "accidents" to describe automobile collisions is highly misleading; it suggests unexpected events. This may be true for individual accidents, but when collisions are viewed from a systemic perspective, the term "accident" is a misnomer. These "accidents" are actually foreseeable events, statistically predictable given the sheer number of cars on the road (Moynihan 1967). No matter how skilled Americans are at driving, there are going to be an enormous number of collisions each year.[12]

What is rare for the individual driver is routine for the system. Former Yale Law School dean and now Circuit Court of Appeals judge Guido Calabresi (1970, 307–08) has noted: "Today accidents must be viewed not as incidental events linking one victim with one injurer, but as a more general societal problem." No fault recognizes—as fault does not—that societal reliance on the automobile carries with it inevitable injury costs. It thus best answers the question: How should the costs be borne?

Nonetheless, the plain fact is that, in their fight against no fault, lawyers have been able to tap into a national reluctance to reform the fault system. The cult of the lawsuit is a powerful one, indeed. For example, a recent survey indicates that a large minority of Americans, almost half, are unwilling to give up their "right to sue" an "at-fault" driver even if doing so allows them to collect full medical expenses and lost wages and save money on premiums (Insurance Research Council 1997).

This reluctance is rooted in a broader conceptual change that has taken place in America's public life: the revolution of "rights." Harvard's Mary Ann Glendon (1991) is one of the astute observers to detect the increasing tendency (since the New Deal and the civil rights movement) of Americans to conceive of almost every social controversy as a "clash of rights." We now tend to see all reforms as either "giving" or "taking" rights (Howard 1994, 116–17; Will 1994, 176).

Given this climate, no fault will always lose the debate over reform so long as it is cast in terms of forcing all to give up the right to sue. Insurance professionals recognize this discouraging fact:

> John Garamendi, California's powerful insurance commissioner, surprised his staff one day by declaring that henceforth, "no fault" insurance would be called "personal-protection" insurance in his office. "What's the difference?" asked an aide at a staff meeting. "About a million votes," replied Walter Zelman, a Garamendi deputy (Yoder 1992).

If this essay accomplishes nothing else, I hope it shows the false premise that no fault takes away people's "rights." In practice, as we have seen, the "right to sue" is really a "right to a lottery ticket." In contrast, true no fault offers accident victims the "right" to immediate, guaranteed compensation and lower insurance premiums.

❑ 6. THE CHOICE SYSTEM

If we had no faults of our own, we should not take so much pleasure in noticing those of others.—*François, Duc de La Rochefoucauld*

Before offering a proposal for improving America's system of automobile insurance, let me repeat why reform is necessary:

1. The fault system is a costly, inefficient, and time-consuming means of compensating accident victims. Attorney fees and other litigation costs drain premium funds away from victim compensation. The remaining funds are off-limits to injured drivers unable to sue. When lawsuits are filed, tort systematically overcompensates victims with minor injuries while undercompensating those with serious ones. In either situation, the cases tend to be slow, clog the courts, and be vulnerable to overstated and fraudulent claims.
2. Lawyers are the primary beneficiaries (and thus defenders) of the current system. Contingency-fee lawyers routinely siphon away a third of an injured person's recovery. Defense attorneys win as soon as a case is filed; they charge by the hour.
3. Insurance costs are driven up by the tort system's promise to compensate victims for their noneconomic damages. These "pain-and-suffering" damages may be real, but they are also impossible to quantify and not available from other insurance. Should we ignore the economic needs of many victims so as to meet the intangible needs of others?
4. The system creates a powerful incentive to inflate damages, typically by claiming unverifiable soft-tissue injuries. The disparity between soft-tissue and hard injuries raises troubling questions about the legitimacy of many payments ultimately passed on to consumers in the form of higher costs.
5. Rampant litigation leads to ever-higher premiums despite ever-safer cars. These skyrocketing costs make auto insurance prohibitively expensive for many urban motorists and are a regressive tax on all

low-income drivers. The problem feeds itself, as more and more Americans behind the wheel are uninsured drivers.

6. The tort system's reliance on the lawsuit saps funds from the public kitty and stymies economic growth. Litigants routinely reach into the "deep pockets" of taxpayers by bringing claims against the government and clogging the courts. Employers now pay more in automobile-liability costs in America than in any other country.

7. The tort system mires accident compensation in a hunt for "fault" even though the search is often fruitless. It spends thousands of dollars per case in lawyer fees and public resources to examine split-second judgments in accidents resembling acts of God.

8. "Add-on" reform of the fault system adds on to the cost of insurance because two policies cover the same injury. Add-on combines high costs and low benefits without curtailing litigation. It is simply the tort system by another name.

9. Monetary thresholds fail to sever the expensive relationship between automobile accidents and litigation. Low thresholds are little better than add-on or tort: The courtroom remains wide open. Higher thresholds simply provide a target at which to aim.

10. Verbal thresholds are more effective, but even here tort claims preserved over the threshold contribute disproportionately to total costs. In addition, lawyers are increasingly adept at scaling them.

So, where do we go from here?

Auto Choice

The optimal solution is clear: the adoption of true no-fault laws. But the unfortunate truth to date is that pure no fault is a political nonstarter. A tension thus exists between the ideal (true no fault) and the real (tort). For too long reform has resulted in "no-fault" statutes that straddle these two poles and are no fault in name only. Litigation has never been extinguished.

But an alternative exists. Recent years have witnessed a growing awareness that compromise no-fault schemes are not the only hope. Instead, the most attractive and politically realistic solution may be the adoption of an insurance alternative commonly known as "auto choice."

Jeffrey O'Connell of the University of Virginia Law School and Michael Horowitz of the Hudson Institute are among the authors of this exit strategy. Simply stated, auto choice unbundles the payments for economic and noneconomic losses and shifts automobile insurance to a first-party, no-fault basis. These two steps allow auto choice to solve (or at least greatly alleviate) many of the problems discussed in this essay.

The auto-choice proposal builds on choice experiments in three no-fault states—Kentucky, New Jersey, and Pennsylvania—that offer an insurance option with no restrictions on lawsuits. Unfortunately, however, none of these states offers drivers a chance to forego expensive pain-and-suffering coverage. But this option is offered in the federal Auto Choice Reform Bill, which was introduced in Congress in early 1999 by bipartisan cosponsors Senators Joseph Lieberman, John McCain, Mitch McConnell, and Daniel Patrick Moynihan. As these distinguished names suggest, auto choice's merits have attracted remarkable bipartisan support.

How It Works

Presently, in forty-seven states, you, the consumer, have absolutely no discretion in deciding the type of automobile insurance to purchase. Your legislature selects whether you and your family will be protected through fault or no-fault insurance. Auto choice gives *you* this ability; it devolves the selection power from the state house to the family house by unbundling the economic and noneconomic components of auto-tort law.

Under auto choice, motorists ("switchers") may buy first-party insurance covering medical costs, lost wages, and rehabilitation expenses. At the same time motorists ("stayers") may remain eligible for pain-and-suffering damages by retaining traditional tort insurance. Thus, motorists have the *choice* of foregoing claims for pain and suffering (hence "auto choice").

Here is how it works: Switchers purchase first-party, no-fault economic coverage at levels required by state law for liability for personal injury. Switchers can neither sue nor be sued for pain-and-suffering damages if involved in an accident with any other motorist, switcher or stayer. Switchers can file tort claims only for economic loss in excess of their first-party (no-fault) coverage. In accidents between switchers and stayers, the latter (who have elected to remain in the tort system) make fault-based claims under "tort maintenance coverage" against their own insurer for pain and suffering much as drivers today file under uninsured motorist coverage. Claims for excess economic losses are allowed against switchers. If two stayers collide, the current tort system operates without change. If drugs or alcohol caused the accident, there is no restriction on anyone's right to sue for pain and suffering.

Auto choice is perhaps best understood as offering elective pain-and-suffering insurance that is available to all but mandatory for none. This unbundling allows switchers to save large amounts of money by not buying traditional tort liability insurance. Even better, it is accomplished via the free market—neither coverage is mandated and drivers are no longer compelled to purchase the same product. This alone is a step in the right direction: "The problem with our current system is that those who pay the premiums . . . have no control over where their money goes" (Berte 1991, 2).

Auto-Choice Benefits   No one knows exactly what the future holds. But we can be fairly certain what will happen if the fault system remains—it will continue to be inadequate, inefficient, and inequitable. On the other hand, if auto choice is implemented, the evidence strongly suggests a future of higher benefits and lower premiums.

The higher benefits flow from auto choice's no-fault nature: Benefits are paid within thirty days to all accident victims (even those of single-car accidents) regardless of fault. The lower costs result from the diminished incentives for fraud and abuse. By precluding suits by or against switchers for pain and suffering, auto choice reduces the number and value of lawsuits while also cutting attorney fees. Money goes to the seriously injured instead of lawyers.

The Rand Corporation, an organization specializing in statistical research that is neutral in the debate over fault versus no fault, has documented dramatic savings under auto choice (Carroll and Abrahamse 1998). Results based on 1992 data indicate that switchers could reduce their personal-injury premiums by a remarkable 45 percent (and their total premium by 20 percent). This estimate varies little with the percentage of switchers. If, say, half of all insured motorists in a tort state are switchers, they will save an average of 20 percent on their total premiums. If everyone switches, the average savings would be 19 percent. (Of course, these averages are just that—averages—and individuals could realize larger or smaller cost savings.) At the same time, savings are not at the expense of those electing to remain under the tort system; their premiums remain the same.

Rand's findings and other insurance industry data form the basis of cost estimates conducted by the staff of the congressional JEC (1998). The JEC estimates that, if enacted, auto choice would have saved over $35.5 billion in 1998 if all drivers elected to switch and $193 billion between 1998 and 2002. According to the JEC, the average switcher would save $184 per year, per car.

These cost savings would help alleviate current stresses imposed by mandatory insurance on low-income drivers. As seen in section 3, tort's high costs saddle the working poor and urban residents with insurance premiums that may eat up as much as one-third of their income. Auto choice offers these motorists a way to obey the law and protect themselves—by purchasing insurance—while not requiring them to go without food in the process. And because low-income motorists cannot afford optional collision and comprehensive property-damage coverages, bodily injury represents a larger share of their overall premium. This allows auto choice to offer them even greater total savings—about 36 percent on average (Joint Economic Committee 1998, 37).

These savings would have the ripple effect of further lowering costs by reducing the number of uninsured motorists. We have seen that when the number of drivers without insurance increases, rates increase—and the percentage in urban areas can exceed 50 percent. By simply reducing the number of drivers without insurance—through the *option* of less expensive no-fault insurance—auto choice will both reduce everyone's rates and protect against accidents with uninsured motorists.

Auto choice does not sacrifice safety on the altar of lower costs. Switchers will still face multiple penalties for bad driving: injury or death, damage to their own cars (not covered by no fault), lawsuits over medical costs and wage losses they cause in excess of the injured party's coverage, suspended driving privileges, criminal sanctions, and increased premiums. Indeed, auto choice may actually *encourage* safety because it will allow insurers to offer discounts for safer cars. These reductions are impossible in a third-party system where (as we have seen) the insurer does not know in advance who will seek payment.

Auto choice is not a panacea. It is instead a creative proposal that allows motorists to opt out of tort's faultfinding and pain and suffering in return for automatic payment for economic loss. Auto choice, in short, allows motorists finally to be in the driver's seat when it comes to selecting insurance. If we fail to embrace it, the fault will be all our own.

ACKNOWLEDGMENTS

I want to thank six people: Don Nichols, Jim Kaster, and Jeff Anderson, who taught me how to practice law; Mike Horowitz and Jeff O'Connell, who taught me how to improve the law; and Rita Simon, who taught me how to write about the law. My essay is dedicated, with love, to my parents, who taught me everything else.

NOTES

1. Judges, as much as anyone, knew early cars were luxuries. In a 1907 decision on a motorist's liability for an accident, *Lewis v. Amorous* (59 S.E. 338, 340

(Ga. Ct. App. 1907)), for example, Georgia jurists complained that "by reason of the rate of pay allotted to judges in this state few, if any, of them have ever owned one of these machines. . . ."

2. But the media should not escape unscathed for the loss of steam of no-fault reform as the 1970s progressed. "Another negative factor since 1974 has been media boredom. A nine-year fight [since 1965] is beyond the attention span of the national and local media. No fault became an old story" (Davies 1998, 846–47).

3. But even this "failure" is not as clear as a summary review makes it appear. A simple state-to-state comparison of premium rates is like comparing apples and oranges. Most no-fault states are urban states that inevitably have more accidents than the rural ones typically held up as exemplars of tort.

4. The underlying concept of insurance—risk distribution—has remained the same since Lloyd's of London began protecting against the loss of a ship and its cargo (Berte 1991). Whether financing a sea voyage or a trip to the corner store, insurance is intended to free individuals from worry about the consequences of being in an accident. A premium payment is the cost of individual risk; everyone pays, the unfortunate collect.

5. Keep in mind that these urban increases are occurring despite new seat-belt laws intended to reduce physical injures in the low-speed crashes common in cities. To note the obvious: These laws should reduce bodily injury claims as a percent of all claims because fewer people are injured in minor collisions.

6. Lawyer-statesman Elihu Root is attributed with a similar, if more forceful, message: "About half the practice of a decent lawyer consists in telling would-be clients that they are damned fools and should stop" (Glendon 1994, 37).

7. This mushrooming helps account for the growth in New York's auto-accident litigation discussed earlier. Between 1987 and 1997, the state's number of lawyers grew twenty-six times faster than its total population (40 percent versus 1.5 percent) (Public Policy Institute 1998, 44).

8. But it should be noted that the promise of no recovery/no fee could be misleading because "fee" does not encompass costs and disbursements. Even losing clients are on the hook for these expenses.

9. Although in one case, as documented by economist Farid Khavari (1990, 180), an "illiterate legal genius had written a contract entitling himself to one-third percent, or 0.0033–1/3 of the settlement."

10. This paragraph condenses a semester of law school into three sentences. For a more detailed discussion about the rise of negligence, I suggest reading the first chapter of Lawrence Friedman's *A History of American Law*. For our purposes, it is enough to note that once there was no negligence, then there was negligence, and now negligence as a legal theory makes little sense in most auto accidents.

11. This concept of the reasonable person is what distinguishes negligence, which is the widest-ranging cause of action, from intentional torts such as assault and battery, where the plaintiff has the more difficult burden of showing deliberate malfeasance on the defendant's part.

12. And this skill level is very much open to question. As Dave Barry has noted, the one thing that unites all Americans is that, deep down inside, we all believe that we are above average drivers.

REFERENCES

Abel, R. L. 1990. "A Critique of Torts." *UCLA Law Review* 37: 785–832.

Bedard, P. 1998. "Auto Insurance Pays Off Big for Crooks and Trial Lawyers." *Car and Driver*, January, 70.

Bell, P. A., and J. O'Connell. 1997. *Accidental Justice: The Dilemmas of Tort Law*. New Haven, Conn.: Yale University Press.

Bernstein, R. 1998. "A Thinker Attuned to Thinking." *New York Times*, 22 August.

Berte, M. M. 1991. *Hit Me—I Need the Money! The Politics of Auto Insurance Reform*. San Francisco: ICS Press.

Bok, D. 1993. *The Cost of Talent: How Executives and Professionals Are Paid and How It Affects America*. New York: Free Press.

Brickman, L. 1994. "On the Relevance of the Admissibility of Scientific Evidence: Tort System Outcomes are Principally Determined by Lawyers' Rates of Return." *Cardozo Law Review* 15: 1755–98.

Brickman, L., M. Horowitz, and J. O'Connell. 1994. *Rethinking Contingency Fees*. New York: The Manhattan Institute.

Calabresi, G. 1970. *The Costs of Accidents: A Legal and Economic Analysis*. New Haven, Conn.: Yale University Press.

Carmen, E. 1919. "Is a Motor Vehicle Accident Compensation Act Advisable?" *Minnesota Law Review* 4: 1–13.

Carroll, S., J. Kakalik, N. Pace, and J. Adams. 1991. *No-Fault Approaches to Compensating People in Automobile Accidents*. Santa Monica, Calif.: Rand Corporation.

Carroll, S., A. Abrahamse, and M. Vaiana. 1995. *The Costs of Excess Medical Claims for Automobile Personal Injuries: Documented Briefing*. Santa Monica, Calif.: Rand Corporation.

Carroll, S., and A. Abrahamse. 1998. *The Effects of a Choice Automobile Insurance Plan on Insurance Costs and Compensation: An Updated Analysis*. Santa Monica, Calif.: Rand Corporation.

Cohen, J. 1999. "Irrational Exuberance." *New Republic*, 25 October, 25–31.

Cramer, R. B. 1992. *What It Takes*. New York: Random House.

Cummins, J. D., and S. Tennyson. 1992. "Controlling Automobile Insurance Costs." *Journal of Economic Perspectives* 6: 95–115.

Davies, J. 1998. "A No-Fault History." *William Mitchell Law Review* 24: 839–47.

Detlefsen, R. R. 1998. *Escaping the Tort-Based Auto Accident Compensation System: The Federal Auto Choice Reform Act of 1997*. Washington, D.C.: Citizens for a Sound Economy Foundation.

Dewees, D., D. Duff, and M. Trebilcock. 1996. *Exploring the Domain of Accident Law: Taking the Facts Seriously*. New York: Oxford University Press.

Dornstein, K. 1996. *Accidentally, On Purpose*. New York: St. Martin's Press.

Easterbrook, G. 1998. "Not Your Average Joe." *New Republic,* 2 November.

Emerson, R. W. 1992. "Insurance Claims Fraud Problems and Remedies." *Miami Law Review* 46: 907–73.

Fitzgerald, J. M. 1999. "Perspectives on Federal Auto Choice Legislation: Comments by Judith M. Fitzgerald." Washington, D.C.: National Insurance Crime Bureau, 28 January. Photocopy.

Foppert, D. 1992. "Does No-Fault Stack Up?" *Best's Review* 92: 2020–26.

Friedman, L. M. 1985. *A History of American Law*. 2d ed. New York: Simon and Schuster.

Galanter, M. 1996. "Real World Torts: An Antidote to Anecdote." *Maryland Law Review* 55: 1093–1160.

Gillespie, P., and M. Klipper. 1972. *No-Fault: What You Save, Gain, and Lose with the New Auto Insurance*. New York: Praeger.

Glendon, M. A. 1991. *Rights Talk: The Impoverishment of Political Discourse*. New York: The Free Press.

———. 1994. *A Nation Under Lawyers: How the Crisis in the Legal Profession Is Transforming American Society*. New York: Farrar, Straus, and Giroux.

Grady, J. F. 1976. "Some Ethical Questions About Percentage Fees." *Litigation* (summer): 20.

Green, L. 1958. *Traffic Victims: Tort Law and Insurance*. Evanston, Ill.: Northwestern University Press.

Greer, D. S. 1992. "No-Fault Compensation for Personal Injuries Arising from Road Accidents: Developments in the U.S." *Anglo-American Law Review* 21: 210–77.

Hager, M. M. 1998. "No-Fault Drives Again: A Contemporary Primer." *University of Miami Law Review* 52: 793–830.

Harper, F. V., F. James, Jr., and O. S. Gray. 1986. *The Law of Torts*. 2d ed. Boston: Little, Brown.

Hensler, D., W. G. Manning, J. A. Rogowski, P. A. Ebener, A. F. Abrahmse, R. J. MacCoun, E. A. Lind, M. S. Marquis, S. H. Berry, and E. G. Lewis. 1991. *Compensation for Accidental Injuries in the United States*. Santa Monica, Calif.: Rand Corporation.

Holmes, O. W. Jr. 1881. *The Common Law*. Boston: Little, Brown.

Hood, J. B., and B. A. Hardy, Jr. 1983. *Workers' Compensation and Employee Protection Laws*. St. Paul, Minn.: West Group.

Horowitz, M. 1998. *Putting Drivers in the Driver's Seat*. Dallas: National Center for Policy Analysis.

Howard, P. K. 1994. *The Death of Common Sense: How Law Is Suffocating America*. New York: Random House.

Hughes, G. 1996. "Common Law Systems." In *Fundamentals of American Law*, edited by A. B. Morrison. New York: Oxford University Press.

Insurance Research Council. 1990. *Trends in Auto Bodily Injury Claims*. Oakbrook, Ill: Insurance Research Council.

————. 1994. *Auto Injuries: Claiming Behavior and Its Impact on Insurance Costs.* Oakbrook, Ill.: Insurance Research Council.

————. 1995. *Public Attitude Monitor 1995.* Oakbrook, Ill.: Insurance Research Council.

————. 1996a. *Fraud and Buildup in Auto Injury Claims: Pushing the Limits of the Auto Insurance System.* Wheaton, Ill.: Insurance Research Council.

————. 1996b. *Trends in Auto Bodily Injury Claims.* Wheaton, Ill: Insurance Research Council.

————. 1997. *Public Attitude Monitor 1997.* Oakbrook, Ill.: Insurance Research Council.

————. 1999. *Paying for Auto Injuries: A Consumer Panel Survey of Auto Accident Victims.* Malvern, Penn.: Insurance Research Council.

James, F. Jr., and S. C. Law. 1952. "Compensation for Auto Accident Victims: A Story of Too Little and Too Late." *Connecticut Bar Journal* 26: 70–81.

Jasper, M. C. 1996. *The Law of No-Fault Insurance.* Dobbs Ferry, N.Y.: Oceana Publications.

Johnston, J. D. 1997. *Driving America: Your Car, Your Government, Your Choice.* Washington, D.C.: AEI Press.

Joint Economic Committee, Congress of the United States. 1996. *Improving the American Legal System: The Economic Benefits of Tort Reform.* Washington, D.C.: Government Printing Office.

————. 1997. *The Benefits and Savings of Auto-Choice.* Washington, D.C.: Government Printing Office.

————. 1998. *Auto Choice: Impact on Cities and the Poor.* Washington, D.C.: Government Printing Office.

Joost, R. H. 1992. *Automobile Insurance and No-Fault Law.* 2d ed. Deerfield, Ill.: Clark Boardman Callaghan.

Jury Verdict Research, Inc. 1993. *Basic Injury Values for Emotional Injuries Resulting from Medical Malpractice and Vehicular Liability.* Horsham, Penn.: LRP Publications.

Keeton, R. E. 1969. *Venturing to Do Justice: Reforming Private Law.* Cambridge, Mass.: Harvard University Press.

Keeton, R. E., and J. O'Connell. 1965. *Basic Protection for the Traffic Victim: A Blueprint for Reforming Automobile Insurance.* Boston: Little, Brown.

Kennedy, R. 1981. "Slashing Contingency Fees." *American Lawyer* 3: 39.

Kerekes, R. 1994. "The Crisis of Congested Courts: One Proposed Solution." *Seton Hall Legislative Journal* 18: 489–551.

Khavari, F. A. 1990. *Vultures: Doctors, Lawyers, Hospitals, and Insurance Companies, What's Wrong, and What to Do About It.* Santa Monica, Calif.: Roundtable Publishing.

King, W. 1970. "'No-Fault' Auto Insurance Is Stalled in Legislatures." *New York Times,* 15 November.

Kionka, E. J. 1977. *Torts in a Nutshell: Injuries to Persons and Property*. St. Paul, Minn.: West Publishing Co.

LaFaive, D. L. 1991. *The Claims Game: How to Play to Win! How to Present, Evaluate, and Settle Your Automobile Injury Claim*. West Hartford, Conn.: Puck and Co. Press.

Landau, N. J. 1979. "The Psychology of the Large Award." In *Proving Damages in Personal Injury Cases*, edited by J. A. Page and W. Baise. Cambridge, Mass.: ATLA Education Fund.

Lasson, K. 1994. "Lawyering Askew: Excesses in the Pursuit of Fees and Justice." *Boston University Law Review* 74: 723–75.

Lee, J. D., and B. A. Lindahl. 1994. *Modern Tort Law: Liability and Litigation*. Rev. ed. Deerfield, Ill.: Clark Boardman Callaghan.

Lewis, S. 1936. "The Merits of the Automobile Compensation Plan." *Law and Contemporary Problems* 3: 583–97.

Lewiston, R. R. 1967. *Hit From Both Sides*. New York: Abelard-Schuman.

Lloyd-Bostock, S. M. 1980. "Common Sense Morality and Accident Compensation." *Insurance Law Journal* (June): 331–45.

Maril, R. L. 1993. "The Impact of Mandatory Auto Insurance upon Low Income Residents of Maricopa County, Arizona." Stillwater: Oklahoma State University. Photocopy.

Marter, S. S., and H. I. Weisberg. 1992. "Medical Expenses and the Massachusetts Automobile Tort Reform Law: A First Review of 1989 Bodily Injury Liability Claims." *Journal of Insurance Regulation* 10: 462–514.

Marx, R. S. 1954. "Reply to 'The Case Against Compulsory Automobile Compensation Insurance.'" *Ohio State Law Journal* 15: 157–60.

Mayer, M. 1980. *The Lawyers*. New York: Harper and Row.

Meeks, J. E. 1998. "Compensating Automobile Accident Victims." In *Automobile Accident Law and Practice*, edited by K. C. Miller, vol. 1. New York: M. Bender.

Mooney, S. 1989. *Auto Insurance: Critical Choices in the 1990s*. New York: Insurance Information Institute.

Morris, C., and J. C. N. Paul. 1962. "The Financial Impact of Automobile Accidents." *University of Pennsylvania Law Review* 110: 913–34.

Moynihan, D. P. 1967. "Next: A New Auto Insurance Policy." *New York Times Magazine*, 27 August.

Nguyen, L. 1996. "Auto Lawsuits Rise, Despite Fewer Accidents." *Washington Post*, 23 June.

Nixon, R. N. 1936. "Changing Rules of Liability in Automobile Accident Litigation." *Law and Contemporary Problems* 3: 476–90.

O'Connell, J. 1971. *The Injury Industry and the Remedy of No-Fault Insurance*. Urbana: University of Illinois Press..

———. 1979. *The Lawsuit Lottery: Only the Lawyers Win*. New York: The Free Press.

O'Connell, J., and C .B. Kelly. 1987. *The Blame Game*. Lexington, Mass.: Lexington Books.

O'Connell, J., S. Carroll, M. Horowitz, and A. Abrahamse. 1993. "Consumer Choice in the Auto Insurance Market." *Maryland Law Review* 52: 1016–62.

O'Connell, J., S. Carroll, M. Horowitz, A. Abrahamse, and D. Kaiser. 1995. "The Costs of Consumer Choice for Auto Insurance in States Without No-Fault Insurance." *Maryland Law Review* 54: 281–351.

Olson, P. L. 1996. *Forensic Aspects of Driver Perception and Response*. Tucson, Ariz.: Lawyers and Judges Publishing Co.

Olson, W. K. 1991. *The Litigation Explosion: What Happened When America Unleashed the Lawsuit*. New York: Truman Talley Books-Dutton.

Peck, C. J. 1970. "Negligence and Liability Without Fault in Tort Law." In *The Origin and Development of the Negligence Action; Studies of the Role of Fault in Automobile Accident Compensation Law: Department of Transportation Automobile Insurance and Compensation Study*. Washington, D.C.: Government Printing Office.

Perlmutter, M. 1997. *Why Lawyers Lie and Engage in Other Repugnant Behavior*. Austin, Tex.: M. Perlmutter.

Posner, G. 1994. *Case Closed: Lee Harvey Oswald and the Assassination of JFK*. New York: Doubleday Books.

Prosser, W. L. 1964. *Handbook of the Law of Torts*. 3d ed. St. Paul, Minn.: West Publishing Co.

Public Policy Institute of New York State. 1998. *An Accident and a Dream*. Albany, N.Y.: Public Policy Institute/Business Council of New York State.

"Reckless Automobilists." 1904. *Central Law Journal*, 59: 432.

Richards, W. C. 1949. *The Last Billionaire*. New York: Charles Scribner's Sons.

Rollins, W. A. 1919. "A Proposal to Extend the Compensation Principle to Accidents in the Streets." *Massachusetts Law Quarterly* 4: 392–96.

Ross, H. L. 1980. *Settled Out of Court: The Social Process of Insurance Claims Adjustments*. New York: Aldine Publishing Co.

Rundlett, E. T., III. 1991. *Maximizing Damages in Small Personal Injury Cases*. Santa Ana, Calif.: James Publishing Group.

Segal, D. 1993. "Crash Cow." *Washington Monthly*, December, pp. 28–32.

"Settling for Less: Applying Law and Economics to Poor People." 1993. *Harvard Law Review* 107: 442–59.

Smith, E., and R. Wright. 1992. "Why Is Automobile Insurance in Philadelphia so Damn Expensive?" *American Economic Review* 82: 756–72.

Spiro, P., and D. Mirvish. 1989. "Whose No-Fault Is It, Anyway?" *Washington Monthly*, October, 24–29.

Sprinkel, E. 1988. *Attorney Involvement in Auto Injury Claims*. Oakbrook, Ill.: All-Industry Research Advisory Council.

Sugarman, S. D. 1989. *Doing Away with Personal Injury Law*. New York: Quorum Books.

Sullivan, E. 1971. *Where Did the $13 Billion Go?* Englewood Cliffs, N.J.: Prentice-Hall.

Taylor, Jr., S. 1998. "How to Save $30 Billion a Year in Car Insurance." *National Journal*, 6 June, 1283–84.

Teaford, J. C. 1990. *The Rough Road to Renaissance: Urban Revitalization in America, 1940–1985.* Baltimore: Johns Hopkins University Press.

Thompson, T. 1991. "Are Attorneys Paid What They're Worth? Contingent Fees and the Settlement Process." *Journal of Legal Studies* 20: 187–223.

Tobias, A. 1993. *Auto Insurance Alert! Why the System Stinks, How to Fix It, and What to Do in the Meantime.* New York: Simon and Schuster.

———. 1997. *My Vast Fortune.* New York: Random House.

U.S. Department of Transportation. 1971. *Motor Vehicle Crash Losses and Their Compensation in the United States: A Report to the Congress and the President.* Washington, D.C.: Government Printing Office.

———. 1985. *Compensating Auto Accident Victims: A Follow-up Report on No-Fault Auto Insurance Experiences.* Washington, D.C.: Government Printing Office.

Viscusi, W. K. 1996. "Pain and Suffering: Damages in Search of a Sounder Rationale." *Michigan Law and Policy Review* 1: 141–78.

Waller, M., and M. A. Hughes. 1999. "Getting There." *The New Democrat*, September/October, 8–10.

Wend, A., T. Britt, M. N. Crislip, D. L. Strickland, and R. Vacante. N.d. *Identifying and Neutralizing No-Fault Legislation: A Field Handbook.* American Trial Lawyers Association.

"Whatever Happened to No-Fault?" 1984. *Consumer Reports*, September, 511–13.

Widiss, A. I., R. R. Bovbjerg, D. D. Cavers, J. W. Little, R. S. Clark, G. E. Waterson, and T. C. Jones. 1977. *No-Fault Automobile Insurance in Action: The Experiences in Massachusetts, Florida, Delaware and Michigan.* Dobbs Ferry, N.Y.: Oceana Publications.

Winfield, P. H. 1926. "The History of Negligence in Torts." *Law Quarterly Review* 57: 184–201.

Will, G. F. 1994. *The Leveling Wind: Politics, the Culture and Other News.* New York: Viking Penguin.

Wilson, J. Q. 1991. *On Character.* Washington, D.C.: AEI Press.

Wolfram, C. W. 1986. *Modern Legal Ethics.* St. Paul, Minn.: West Publishing Co.

Yoder, S. K. 1992. "Insurance Regulator in California Woos Voters, Bashes Firms." *Wall Street Journal*, 10 August.

Zekman P., and G. Mustain. 1980. "The Accident Swindlers." *Chicago Sun-Times*, 10 February.

PART THREE

Responses

Rejoinder

Jerry J. Phillips

I was at a conference in Connecticut in the spring of 2000, where we discussed the controversial issue of handgun control in the United States. Statistical data flowed in all directions on every issue, and I must say I felt awash in the data.

We all know the quip that there are lies, damned lies, and statistics. But in Connecticut I got a new twist on statistical data: Even assuming your data are correct, what conclusions should you properly draw from that data (Davies 1999, 750)?

The point was graphically illustrated through a grisly story told by one of the presenters at the conference. He said once there was a famous scientist who was studying communication with grasshoppers. The scientist thought he had finally learned to communicate with his grasshopper. When he slapped the table on which his grasshopper was perched and shouted "jump!", the grasshopper would jump.

To test his hypothesis, the scientist pulled one of the wings off his grasshopper, replaced the hapless hopper on the table, and gave his command to jump. The grasshopper jumped, but not so well as before.

Making notes, he continued his experiments. Off with the second wing, command, and still weaker jump. Off with one leg, command, and yet a weaker jump. Off with both legs, command, and no movement at all from the hapless grasshopper.

The famous scientist noted in his little book: "When wings and legs of grasshopper are removed, grasshopper apparently loses sense of hearing."

So it is with the data on auto tort and auto no fault. Let us assume, for example, that lawyers' fees just about equal the amount of payout to claimants on the auto liability insurance dollar. What are we to make of that? Should lawyers go unpaid? Even better, should we kill all the lawyers, as Dick the Butcher proposed (*Henry VI*, pt. 2, Act 4, sc. 2; Phillips 1999, 795)?

My friend Steve Chippendale quotes in section 2 of his presentation herein a British lawyer named Greer, who opines that "the general verdict in the United States does appear to be that no-fault has been a success in Michigan and New York." The English, you will recall, are the ones who have abolished the right to trial by jury, which is enshrined in our federal and state constitutions. The "general verdict" that Greer refers to, "in" the United States, is apparently not that "of" the United States.

Harvey Rosenfield (1998, 88) states in his *University of Memphis Law Review* article that in 1995 New York had the fifth-highest average auto insurance premiums in the nation. Rosenfield quotes a Michigan study indicating that during the period 1977–89, a total of 73 percent of the appellate opinions in Michigan "were first party cases in which insureds were suing their own insurance company to obtain no-fault benefits." And he quotes a Michigan representative, who testified before Congress that the "number of first party auto no-fault lawsuits filed in Michigan is nearly three times as great as the number of third party suits" (Rosenfield 1998, 100–101). It's those pesky lawyers again.

My friend Steve rightly notes that the impetus for no-fault auto insurance began with a comparison to the no-fault system of workers' compensation. But workers' compensation has never been a bed of roses in this country. The amount of payout is politically controlled, and has typically been woefully inadequate. Jonathan Weisgall (1977, 1038–39) noted a study in 1976–77, which showed that products liability claims arising out of workplace injuries accounted for 42 percent of products-liability, bodily-injury payments. All cannot be happy in the workplace no-fault compensation area, where there is that kind of pressure to return to the tort system.

An interesting analogue about workers' compensation in this country is the history of the Federal Employers Liability Act, familiarly known as FELA (Phillips 1993, 1063). When workers' compensation began to sweep this country in the early part of the twentieth century, the railroad barons—who then represented one of the most powerful industries in the nation—set about to use its tremendous political influence to stave off the adoption of a socialistic workers' compensation program for railroad employees. The result was the enactment by Congress of FELA, a statutory tort system of recovery for railroad employees against their employers.

The railroads soon saw their error in promoting FELA, which proved more costly than the meager benefits of the typical workers' compensation program. But by the time they realized their mistake it was too late to substitute workers' compensation for FELA, because the railroad employees liked FELA and their unions had become politically strong enough to fight off repeal. Repeated efforts on the part of the railroads during the twentieth century to repeal FELA have met with repeated failures.

The FELA history presents an interesting parallel to that of the attitude of the insurance industry toward no-fault auto insurance in this country. As Steve points out (section 2), the insurance industry was opposed to the adoption of no fault when it was initially proposed—undoubtedly because they thought no fault would be more costly than tort. Now the tables are turned, and the insurance industry is one of the foremost proponents of no fault (Rosenfield 1998).

Workplace tort litigation is a burgeoning industry today—for example, from sex and race discrimination claims, to age discrimination, employee disability, and wrongful discharge claims. These are all tort claims, brought outside the personal-injury jurisdiction of workers' compensation. It's those pesky lawyers again.

My friend Steve in section 2 of his presentation bemoans the fact that no-fault add-on benefits "help finance lawsuits because the up-front payments *allow plaintiffs to wait during litigation*" (emphasis added). It strikes me as eminently fair that plaintiffs *should* be able to wait during litigation. Unless of course you happen to believe that litigation is bad. I think it is good. Or rather, I think it is good that that avenue of rights protection is available. The vast majority of auto-tort claims settle. For those that do not, where there is a genuine dispute that cannot be settled by negotiation, then fairness demands that a judicial remedy be made available.

Steve says in his introductory material that one of the experiences that helped convince him that no fault is a good thing was his experience as a teenager while working in the drivers license division of the Missouri Department of Revenue and seeing "the ease with which almost everyone obtains, and renews, their licenses. . . ." I by no means advocate tort law as the sole sanction against careless driving. I think licenses should be harder to obtain than they are. I think cars should be mandatorily inspected for safety at least once a year. I think criminal sanctions for speeding, for driving while drunk, and for other safety violations should be strictly enforced. But I do not believe any of these other sanctions provides a substitute for the deterrence of tort law. I certainly do not believe that no fault provides such a substitute.

At the beginning of his section 3, my friend quotes the allegedly truthful statistic that "[a]bout one-third of claimed medical costs are excessive and unnecessary." That is like saying that claims for pain and suffering are excessive and unnecessary. We are all aware of the major debate in this country today about the high price of medical care on the one hand, and whether, on the other hand, the cost-containment practices of health maintenance organizations are counterproductive. I do not see how either auto tort or no fault provides any remedy to the major problems of medical costs in this country, although I do believe that tort law is necessary to promote medical care just as it is necessary to promote driver care.

Steve makes the subtle leap in section 3 from the purpose of auto insurance to the purpose of auto-tort liability. He states that the purpose of insurance is to compensate, and then says tort law achieves that purpose very inadequately. But of course the purpose of tort law is also to deter, and the compensatory-deterrent goals of tort law are in constant tension.

As has been often noted, the availability of liability insurance tends to undermine the deterrent goal of tort law. But merit rating of liability insurance based on accidents caused by the fault of the insured will help correct this problem. Insurance aside, a finding of fault has a therapeutic effect both for the tortfeasor and for the victim.

Based on data set forth in his Table 2, Steve asserts that auto victims with more than $100,000 in economic damages recover in tort on average "just nine percent of their loss." Apparently he is referring here to victims who have a valid tort claim against a tortfeasor with inadequate liability insurance. This finding, if correct, strongly suggests that the requirement of compulsory auto liability insurance with reasonably high limits of coverage should be rigorously enforced.

Citing Joost (1992), Steve states that in the "typical year" of 1993 "one-car accidents constituted 59.9 percent of all fatal accidents and 32.1 percent of all injury-causing accidents. . ." The victims of these accidents have no one to sue in tort, he laments. What he does not say is how many of these accidents involved drinking, drug use, and other wanton misconduct for which no-fault insurance would provide no coverage either. As noted in section 2 of my presentation, a presumably typical New York study indicated that 77 percent of the drivers killed in single-car accidents had been drinking.

Steve points out the high price of auto liability insurance. But what is the cause of that? Rosenfield's informed study of the California situation, discussed in my section 5, indicates that much of the problem lies with unregulated, excessive practices of the insurance companies themselves. If the grasshopper does not jump when commanded, we should not assume the reason is that the grasshopper cannot hear. Nor should we assume that high insurance rates are invariably caused by those pesky lawyers. The so-called liability insurance crises of the 1970s and 1980s in this country put the lie to that assumption.

In his section 4, Steve laments the fact that, while automobile personal injury accidents have experienced a decline in this country over the past couple of decades, the number of auto-tort claims has experienced a significant increase. Again, what do we make of this phenomenon? He concludes that the increase is "because the tort system lures many accident 'victims' (and their lawyers) to seek easy money." Or, perhaps, it is because litigants have become more aware of their rights.

Paul Weiler et al. (1993, 62) noted a 1970s California study indicating that "for every ten negligent adverse events—that is, instances of torts—actually occurring within the California health-care system, only one malpractice claim was lodged." Suppose the number of medical injuries declined by, let us say 50 percent, but the number of persons asserting malpractice claims from such injuries increased by 50 percent. A logical conclusion to me would be that more people had become aware of their rights. The same is true with auto-tort claims.

Steve asserts that a 1992 study indicated that one out of every three auto-accident personal-injury claims "appeared" to involve "padding or outright fraud." Does he think that fraud does not occur, for instance, in pure no-fault environments such as workers' compensation in the United States, or under the pure no-fault scheme of New Zealand? Studies indicate that fraud is widespread in these areas. Surely Steve does not think that fraud is within the special bailiwick of auto-tort claims.

"The law," as Steve points out (quoting a federal district court case), "dictates no method of calculating pain and suffering damages," except, as Kip Viscusi concedes, the "enlightened conscience" of the jury. Tort law in general, and its damages aspects in particular, relies heavily on the enlightened conscience of the jury. I find that fact highly reassuring, rather than disconcerting. When we stop relying on the "enlightened conscience" of the average citizen, we will be in deep trouble.

My criticisms of the choice system, which Steve advocates in his final section, are contained in section 7 of my presentation. I must say that the choice system sounds a little bit like a current political proposal to allow social security recipients to choose between investment in the public or the private system of retirement security. In the case of social security, the affluent will likely jump ship, leaving the less well-off to go down. In the case of auto no-fault choice, the high-risk drivers would jump ship, leaving the tort electors no tort remedy against those risky drivers who cause the accidents.

I think Steve Chippendale's position—as well as that of many no-fault advocates—can be summed up in his statement in his section 4 on the role of lawyers. "The fundamental flaw with the current system," he says, "is that lawyers control it."

I realize that lawyer bashing has long been a popular sport—though seldom one engaged in by a lawyer himself as in Steve's case.

I realize that there are bad lawyers out there, just as there are bad judges, bad doctors, bad insurers, bad cops, and bad people in general. But I, for one, am not ready to chuck the tort system—either in automobile accidents, or in general—just because some abuse the system. I have seen too many good things come out of the tort system—things that the government was unable, or unwilling, to tackle. Tort lawyers brought down the asbestos industry. They are in the midst of dismantling the tobacco industry. They brought the Dalkon Shield manufacturer to bay, as well as the silicone-gel breast implant industry, and many others. They will be the ones to attack the enormous problems of environmental and toxic pollution in the twenty-first century.

I am fully aware of the faults of the jury system. But I do not see any satisfactory substitute. I am fully aware of the faults of democracy, but I do not see any satisfactory substitute there either.

As a legal academician, I am all too fully aware of the faults of the legal profession. We are likely to sell our soul to mammon, just as society as a whole is likely to do so. But there are still quite a few of those lawyers out there like Atticus Finch in Harper Lee's *To Kill A Mockingbird*. Those lawyers can be found in generous numbers in the area of plaintiffs' tort law.

REFERENCES

Davies, T. Y. 1999. "Recovering the Original Fourth Amendment." *Michigan Law Review* 98: 547–50.

Joost, R. H. 1992 supplement. 2d ed. *Automobile Insurance and No-Fault Law.* Deerfield, Ill.: Clark, Boardman, Callaghan.

Phillips, J. J. 1993. "FELA Revisited." *Maryland Law Review* 52: 1063–69.

Rosenfield, H. 1998. "Auto Insurance: Crisis and Reform." *University of Memphis Law Review* 29: 69–135.

Weiler, P. C., H. H. Hiatt, J. P. Newhouse, W. G. Johnson, T. A. Brennan, and L. L. Leape. 1993. *A Measure of Malpractice: Medical Injury, Malpractice Litigation, and Patient Compensation.* Cambridge, Mass.: Harvard University Press.

Weisgall, J. M. 1977. "Product Liability in the Workplace: The Effects of Workers' Compensation on the Rights and Liabilities of Third Parties." *Wisconsin Law Review* 1977, no. 4: 1035–88.

Rejoinder
Stephen Chippendale

This book puts automobile insurance on trial. Because the case for the prosecution is so overwhelming—waste, fraud, and delay—the current system needs a highly skilled defender. Fortunately for fault, it has found just such an advocate: Jerry Phillips.

Jerry's graceful essay marshals the evidence to cast the best possible light on the current system. And, indeed, we agree on several issues. We both believe that the key issue is how best to compensate the injured. We agree that automobiles can pose a significant threat to public safety and that too many cars are operated by financially irresponsible drivers. Jerry and I also agree that, regardless of no fault's merits, serious political obstacles stand in the way of fundamental reform. We both believe, in short, that U.S. auto insurance is a subject worthy of further scrutiny by *both* scholars and policymakers.

But this would be a dull book if its coauthors were of one mind. And, of course, our essays reflect the fact that we hold significantly different views about how best to achieve the common goal of compensating accident victims. Jerry renews the vows between tort and auto insurance; I propose a divorce.

Our contradictory conclusions are woven from many threads. My essay, for example, reflects a belief that the current system forces Americans to purchase expensive insurance that too often provides inefficient, inadequate, and inequitable coverage. It argues that the system, with its incentives to sue, is not only expensive and slow, but it also promotes fraud and abuse. Jerry, on the other hand, either disagrees with these conclusions or finds, on balance, greater flaws to exist with no-fault reform.

A point-by-point rejoinder would swallow my earlier essay, unfairly tax readers and editors, and threaten the indigenous tree population. Instead, I propose to spend my few remaining pages on what I see as the three principal questions that Jerry raises in his defense of liability insurance: (1) Does no fault raise the risks of motoring by removing a important deterrent to unsafe driving, the lawsuit? (2) Does tort do a superior job of compensating accident victims? (3) Does "add-on" insurance present the optimal solution? Jerry's essay posits that the questions, each of which goes to the heart of the debate, are answered in the affirmative. I want to suggest again that "no" is a better answer.

❏ NO FAULT AND DETERRENCE

I freely admit that the burden of proof falls on me—an advocate of no fault—when the debate turns to the question of whether substitution of no-fault coverage will increase accidents due to decreased care in driving. After all, I do not suggest that lawsuits harm the quality of driving. The issue, instead, is whether tort is responsible for an automobile-accident rate that Jerry and I both agree is falling.

I am highly skeptical of tort's ability to claim credit for our safer roads. As I explained in section 5, deterrence against unsafe driving is best seen as being affected by a combination of criminal and tort sanctions, as well as (and probably above all) a driver's self-interest in protecting her body and property. Regardless of the insurance system in place, reckless drivers risk life and limb—a lawsuit is not an airbag. (This self-preservation distinguishes accident litigation from, say, contract claims where the deterrence value of a potential claim carries more force.) And regardless of the insurance system, reckless drivers risk higher premiums and criminal prosecutions.

My suspicion that tort, alone, is not responsible for the reduced accident rate also stems from the fact that the tort system has been in place since the Model T. As discussed in my section 2, lawsuits have always been the dominant method of compensating accident victims; this was true when the accident rate was high, and it remains true today. In other words, with respect to litigation, little or nothing has changed. If tort wants responsibility for today's safer roads, it must also, I think, accept blame for the days when collisions and fatalities were more prevalent.

What has changed, however, is the quality of our vehicles. Antilock brakes, to name just one technological innovation, have probably saved more lives in recent years than any lawsuit. Moreover, these technological advances have been buttressed by public policy initiatives such as the highly successful campaign against drunk driving. Tort has nothing to do with these safety measures, and no fault would not roll them back.

Jerry cites empirical studies that purport to show that no fault produces higher accident rates. For the reasons above, I am not convinced. Furthermore, as American University's Mark Hager (1998, 811–16) recently noted, the methods used in these studies have been called into question. Elizabeth Landes (1982, 50), for example, contended that curtailing fault increases reckless driving. But her study failed to control for such variables as weather, road quality, and driver training. Other scholars have redone Landes's study with a different (and superior) statistical model and discredited the earlier result. This fresh finding that no fault does not increase accidents is supported by a U.S. Department of Transportation study (1985, 6) that compared no fault with tort states and found no statistically significant difference in the fatality and injury rates.

Stephen Sugarman (1989, 22–23) puts his finger on another reason for viewing these studies with suspicion: The researchers are incapable of providing proof that drivers become less safe when lawsuits are limited. The studies instead are limited to showing, at best, that when driving becomes less expensive, Americans drive more, and, ergo, have more accidents. But this conclusion falls outside the debate over no fault. The studies suggest that perhaps we should consider steps (e.g., increased registration fees) that would make motoring more expensive, but they shed no light on the quality of driving by those who do get behind the wheel.

A final word: Jerry's essay praises "merit-rating" insurance schemes whereby a driver's safety record is reflected in her insurance premiums. This is another patch of common ground. But I see merit rating as another reason for supporting the adoption of no fault generally and the "auto-choice" system described in section 6 specifically. Auto choice allows superior calibration of premiums and safety because, as a first-party system, it provides insurers with advance knowledge about the identity of the person who would make a claim under the policy. Auto choice, for example, will allow insurers to offer discounts for safer cars—a reduction impossible in the current third-party, liability system where the insurer does not know who may seek payment. In other words, instead of undermining safety, no fault (and auto choice) will actually promote it.

❏ NO FAULT AND COMPENSATION

With the issue of deterrence, I acknowledged that the burden fell on me to show why no-fault reform does not threaten the happy trend of reduced automobile accidents. But when attention turns to compensation, the tables are turned. The burden of proof, I think, now falls on Jerry (and other tort defenders) to show that the current system is not fatally flawed when it comes to recompensing accident victims. There can be little real doubt that no fault exceeds tort's ability to provide effective compensation. As Mark Hager (1998, 806) notes: "In general, studies have found existing no fault schemes superior to tort for rational and efficient delivery of compensation. This is unsurprising, since the chief inspiration for no fault is the deficiency of tort as a compensation system."

Before proceeding any further, let me reiterate an important point: Jerry and I agree that accident victims deserve compensation. Neither of us advocates leaving the injured out in the cold. It's just that the devil is in the details, and two in particular: increased liability limits and pain-and-suffering damages.

Regarding increased liability limits, Jerry observes, and correctly so, that recovery in tort varies dramatically depending on if the other driver has adequate liability insurance. Indeed, a plurality of states require limits of only $20,000 per individual and $40,000 per accident. The next largest number set their limits at $15,000 and $30,000, respectively. Jerry and I agree that these low limits impair full compensation.

Where we part company is on what should be done. Jerry proposes raising the limits as high as $500,000. But my essay suggests that such an increase (which would also raise premiums) would not solve the problem, and may even exacerbate it. Our contrasting conclusions flow from different underlying assumptions. Jerry suggests that, besides making more money available to victims, the higher costs will reduce the number of financially irresponsible (and often reckless) drivers. By contrast, while I agree that only the fully insured should drive, I think that it is a mistake to assume that if someone cannot afford automobile insurance that person will not drive.

Recall the discussion in section 3 about how (too) many drivers today flout the current low limits imposed by state legislatures. In some areas, as we saw, estimates of uninsured drivers range as high as 50 percent—every other motorist—and can reach 90 percent in some urban areas. California alone, for example, is estimated to have over five million uninsured drivers (Joint Economic Committee 1998, 17). The reality, I think, is that these numbers will only go up (and up) if we further increase the price of liability insurance. More victims would then find themselves injured by people who lack the wherewithal to compensate them.

A further problem is that the initial price hike needed to cover higher limits would only be the beginning of premium increases. Smith and Wright (1992, 759) have described how the uninsured-motorist problem feeds itself. As premiums rise to offset the costs of higher coverage, fewer people pay nothing into the insurance pool while retaining full litigation rights in the case of an accident. If mandatory limits were raised, the Smith and Wright cycle would increase costs even more and lead, in turn, to a growth in the number of uninsured drivers. (And, of course, increased liability limits would do nothing to plug the current compensation holes—for example, one-car accidents—that exist in the tort system.) In short, it is my belief that we should be seeking to make insurance more affordable, not more expensive.

Regarding pain-and-suffering damages, Jerry makes a forceful case that (1) what he calls "dignitary injuries" are real and (2) providing recovery for them is worth driving up the cost of auto insurance. As for point 1, there is no quarrel from me that these injuries exist—many victims suffer a loss of enjoyment of life. I could also agree with point 2 if we had an unlimited pool of insurance proceeds. But, as we have seen, accident victims with over $25,000 in out-of-pocket losses recover, on average, only a third of their losses. Financial limits exist, and they impose the necessity of difficult policy decisions.

These financial constraints require us to make a choice between using insurance proceeds to compensate actual pecuniary loss or speculative psychic loss. O'Connell and Kelly (1987, 119) sketch the choice that confronts us:

> [T]he "pain and suffering" endured by the victim of any accident is, at best, difficult to translate into a dollar figure; indeed, the worse the suffering, the more sadly inadequate monetary compensation of any kind seems. And what about the "pain and suffering" endured by accident victims . . . who can't blame their fate on someone else? Should their economic needs go unmet while we grope to meet the less tangible needs of others? If we are going to spend money on suffering people, shouldn't we put a priority on problems we *can* solve, such as unpaid medical bills?

Why should economic needs go unmet? They shouldn't—particularly when (as we have seen) most pain-and-suffering payments end up in the pockets of those with niggling injuries and, consequently, the least pain.

Rather than allowing these people to profit from their accidents, by paying them more than they lost, the system should pay bills and reimburse lost wages for *everyone*. If it does, auto insurance can—at long last—prevent financial catastrophe (which is, after all, the true purpose of any insurance) and discourage those who would bring inflated and even fraudulent claims for alleged pain and suffering.

Jerry and I thus stand on different sides of the pitched battle over payments for psychic loss. But war is avoidable—auto choice offers an armistice. In section 6, I described how this new reform offers elective pain-and-suffering insurance that is available to all but mandatory for none. Under auto choice, motorists who want to save money (known as "switchers") may buy first-party insurance limited to medical costs and lost wages. These drivers are also immune to pain-and-suffering claims. On the other hand, motorists who want to remain eligible for pain-and-suffering damages ("stayers") may retain traditional tort insurance—and recover their psychic loss. And finally, any driver can sue or be sued for pain and suffering if an accident results from drug or alcohol abuse or intentional misconduct.

Auto choice, in short, uses the free market to remove the divisive topic of pain and suffering from the realm of academic discourse and makes it a pocketbook issue. Do you want the ability to recover your psychic loss? If so, pay for it. If not, pocket the savings. A positive by-product of this choice is that it eases the financial pressure imposed on low-income drivers by mandatory insurance requirements. It will also reduce the number of uninsured motorists—fewer people will have to choose between food and insurance.

❏ ADD-ON IS NOT A CHOICE SYSTEM

As the above suggests, Jerry's assessment of auto insurance departs most sharply from mine when we turn to the subject of costs. Simply put, he wants to make insurance expansive; I want to make it inexpensive.

These contrasting emphases are probably never more evident than when we sketch our proposed alternatives to the current state of affairs. I champion auto choice, with its low costs and free-market nature. Jerry finds this reform to be deficient in several respects. His ideal system would be an add-on system that combines no-fault benefits with unlimited lawsuits. But section 2 of my essay argues that add-on simply adds on to the cost of insurance because two policies cover the same injury. In other words, what Jerry calls the best system, I see as the worst.

This striking disjuncture stems in large part from the value we assign to—and what we are willing to pay for—"corrective justice." Unlike Jerry, I find it (at least for automobile accidents) to have limited appeal—and to be unworthy of high premiums. My essay touches upon this topic several times, but it is so important that I want to end my comments by returning to it a final time.

Corrective justice is a fancy term for the fairness of exacting compensation from a culpable party (Hager 1998, 802). And Jerry is surely right that it is a mistake for would-be reformers to simply dismiss the idea that tort law—and thus the current insurance system—provides corrective justice. The themes of retribution and restitution, after all, are at the heart of the criminal law and provide the motivation for most civil suits. But again, the question is: At what cost?

Section 3 documented the high costs of the auto-tort system. Take rampant litigation, add fraudulent and inflated claims, sprinkle in high uninsured-motorist rates, sauté that with expensive lawyers, and you have a recipe for expensive inefficiency. All of the above has motorists reaching ever deeper into their (none-too-deep) pockets: Liability premiums have grown at about twice the rate of inflation over the past two decades.

The bad news—there's precious little good news—is that against these debits can be placed a sole credit: corrective justice. Yet, as with pain-and-suffering compensation, corrective justice is at best an intangible that must be weighed against the tangible problems arising from the current system. Furthermore, the concept becomes even more nebulous when one considers that we are talking about accidental car collisions rather than intentional crimes. What "injustice" needs to be corrected?

Yes, obviously the injured need to be made whole. But no fault does this more rationally and effectively than tort. The current system's single claim to justice superiority, then, is that it extracts a pound of flesh from defendants. But this justification, to my mind, is little more than Swiss cheese. First and foremost, in cases involving accidental collisions, it does not make sense to describe auto-accident litigation as "correcting" the damage inflicted by "guilty" defendants upon "innocent" plaintiffs. Again, these defendants did not commit cold-blooded murder; they had the misfortune to be involved in something they would have rather avoided. "Human failures in a machine age cause a large and fairly regular . . . toll of life, limb, and property. The most important aspect of these failures is not their moral quality; frequently they involve little or nothing in the way of personal moral shortcoming" (Harper, James, and Gray 1986, 132).

We are all fallible—you should see my spelling, for example—and accidents will occur, particularly when vehicles weighing several thousand pounds are propelled at speeds exceeding sixty miles per hour. Indeed, motoring mistakes, as we have seen, are almost ubiquitous and accidents have a random quality. There is thus relatively little culpability—that is, need to censure—in most accident cases. And regardless, it is insurance underwriters—not the defendants themselves—who actually pay the vast bulk of auto-tort claims.

Corrective justice, in the end, is a notion that defies empirical analysis. Jerry is willing to pay for it at the expense of compensation rationality. I am not. Auto choice allows you to decide for yourself.

REFERENCES

Hager, M. M. 1998. "No-Fault Drives Again: A Contemporary Primer." *University of Miami Law Review* 52: 793–830.

Harper, F. V., F. James, Jr., and O. S. Gray. 1986. *The Law of Torts*. 2d ed. Boston: Little, Brown.

Joint Economic Committee. 1998. *Auto Choice: Impact on Cities and the Poor.* Washington, D.C.: Government Printing Office.

Landes, E. 1982. "Insurance, Liability, and Accidents: A Theoretical and Empirical Investigation of the Effects of No-Fault Accidents." *Journal of Law and Economics* 25: 49–65.

O'Connell, J., and C .B. Kelly. 1987. *The Blame Game*. Lexington, Mass.: Lexington Books.

Smith, E., and R. Wright. 1992. "Why Is Automobile Insurance in Philadelphia so Damn Expensive?" *American Economic Review* 82: 756–72.

Sugarman, S. D. 1989. *Doing Away with Personal Injury Law*. New York: Quorum Books.

U.S. Department of Transportation. 1985. *Compensating Auto Accident Victims: A Follow-up Report on No-Fault Auto Insurance Experiences*. Washington, D.C.: Government Printing Office.

Index

Justice Statistics, U.S. Bureau of
  auto tort cases, percentage of civil
    cases, 23, 27
  recovery in litigation, 15
  time to payment, 28

Kakalick, J. S., 21
Kalven, Harry, Jr., 10, 15, 30
Keeton, Robert E.
  auto property claims, 27
  claims financing, 29–30
  insurance premium rating, 36n5
  no-fault insurance proposal, 3, 16,
    35n1, 55–57
  uninsured drivers, 16
Kelly, C. B., 121
Khavari, Farid, 99n9
"Kids on the Go," 71–72
Kimball, Spencer L., 10

Labor Statistics, U.S. Bureau of, cost of
    automobile insurance, 66
LaFaive, Douglas, 78
Landes, Elizabeth, 13, 119
lawyers
  car-accident litigation and, 81–86
  political influence of, 58–59
  tort system and, 114
Lewis v. Amorous, 98–99n1
liability insurance, 12–13, 15–16, 26,
    65–66, 112–13
Licari v. Elliot, 61
Lieberman, Joseph, 96
Lincoln, Abraham, 82
litigation
  attitude toward, 111
  claim padding, 75–80
  growth of and claims rates, 72–74
  insurance fraud, 75, 80–81
  lawyers' role in, 81–86
  right to sue, 93–94
  temptation and, 74–75
Little, Joseph, 13–14
Lloyd-Bostock, Sally, 91–92
Lloyd's of London, 99n4
low-income drivers
  high insurance costs and, 69–71

uninsured, 67–68

The Magnificent Ambersons (Wells),
    51
Mandell, Mark, 22
Maril, Robert, 69–70
Marryott, Franklin J., 6
Massachusetts
  claims in, 76–77
  no-fault insurance, initiation of,
    56–57
  Pinnick v. Cleary, 27
  threshold no-fault insurance, 60
McCain, John, 96
McConnell, Mitch, 96
media, no-fault insurance and,
    99n2
merit rating, 13, 119
Michigan
  claims in, 76
  threshold no-fault insurance, 61
Morris, Clarence, 15
Moynihan, Daniel Patrick, 96

National Safety Council, 23
negligence
  automobiles, application to, 88–89
  origins and meaning of, 86–88
  See also fault, determination of
Neuwirth, Gloria S., 15
New York
  lawyers in, 99n7
  threshold no-fault insurance, 61
New Zealand, 3
Nixon, Richard, 90
no-fault insurance
  auto-choice proposal, 95–98,
    113–14, 119, 122
  compensation under (see
    compensation)
  cost issues (see costs)
  current status of, 59–62
  forms of, 3–4, 30–34
  insurance deterrence effect and, 13
  origins and history of, 53–59
  societal values and, 14
  superiority of, 45–47, 49–51